NO NONSENSE

FLY FISHING GUIDEBOOKS

Bill Mason

Fly Fishing Idaho

A Quick, Clear Understanding of Where to Fly Fish in Idaho

NO NONSENSE

FLY FISHING GUIDEBOOKS

Author
Bill Mason

Maps, Illustrations, and Production
Pete Chadwell, *Dynamic Arts*
Gary D. Smith, *Performance Design*

Front Cover Photo
Steve Bly

Editors
Jim Yuskavitch and David Banks

Published By
No Nonsense Fly Fishing Guidebooks
P.O. Box 91858
Tucson AZ 85752-1858
www.nononsenseguides.com

Printed in USA

Disclaimer
While this guide will greatly help fly fishers, it is not a substitute for caution, good judgment, and the services of a qualified fly fishing guide or outfitter.

ISBN-10 1-892469-17-0
ISBN-13 978-1-892469-17-5

Previous Edition ISBN 0-9637256-1-0

No Nonsense Fly Fishing Guidebooks believes that in addition to local information and gear, fly fishers need clean water and healthy fish. The publisher encourages preservation, improvement, conservation, enjoyment, and understanding of our waters and their inhabitants. A good way to do this is to support organizations dedicated to these ideas.

Acknowledgments

The author thanks the following people for their assistance and comments during this guide's production: My word processor friends Becky and Linda. The great fly fishing experts I've known. Author of the first No Nonsense guide, Harry Teel, and his word processing wife, Dee. David Banks, who came up with the idea and put things together. Lynn Perrault who made my maps tidy and designed covers on the previous edition. Steve Bly for his photographs. The contributions of these people were of immeasurable value. Thanks to all of you.

Rainbow Trout.

Dedication

This guide is dedicated to my loving wife, Jane, my son, Hank, and my daughter, Olivia.

With these people in my life, pursuimg rising trout has become less important than it once was.

My family has made me more fully aware that there is a great deal more to life than fly fishing.

Foreword

Throughout most of my adult life, I have been the envy of many people, for most think I have had the perfect job. Not only have I taught thousands to cast and fly fish, I have done so on some of the great river systems in Idaho and throughout the world. Not every day has been rosy, and at times my career has been financially frightening. But I must admit that, for 25 years, my job has been more satisfying than most conventional occupations.

Putting together a book of this type has been fun and I hope proves rewarding for not only the out of state angler wishing to fish Idaho, but for many Idahoans as well. Unfortunately, it is this type of book that can breed controversy, inspiring spirited conversations and debate.

During my professional career, I have averaged more than 150 days a year on various body of waters, primarily in Idaho. Even with this amount of angling time, no fisherman (including myself), knows everything about every stream or lake that the state has to offer. Obviously, some people will disagree as to the rankings, placement and even non-placement of the waters presented, for I have yet to see the day when anglers, especially fly fishermen, would agree

on much of anything. I guess that's why we call it fishing. I have tried to be totally honest about each body of water. If I have had limited experience, or relied on outside information, I will point it out. Conditions do change, and one should take this book as merely a guide and not the gospel last word. Because of this, it is imperative to seek out local information from those people who fish a particular stream or lake on a daily or regular basis. Their knowledge can be indispensable.

A quick note on the ratings. Each system has been rated from 1–10, with 10 the highest and 1 fishable, but not much else. The ratings are based on my experience which may not coincide with the experience of others. Therefore, the ratings should be used only as a general guide, depending on certain circumstances.

Finally, I hope the information found throughout the pages of this book will be useful not only in determining where to cast a fly, but how and when to fish the waters selected. Fly fishing Idaho can be a magnificent experience, and my hope is that this book only adds to the splendor.

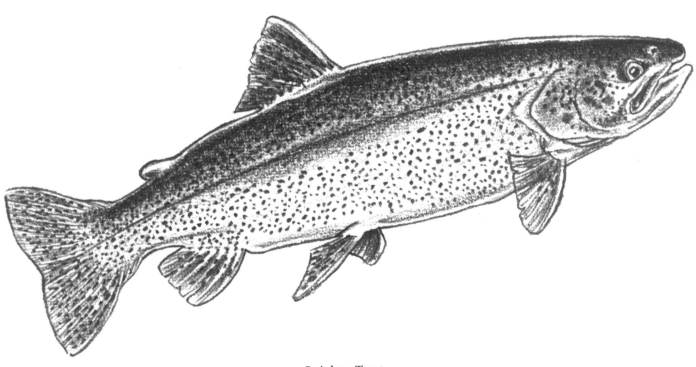

Rainbow Trout.

Contents

Idaho Vicinity Map

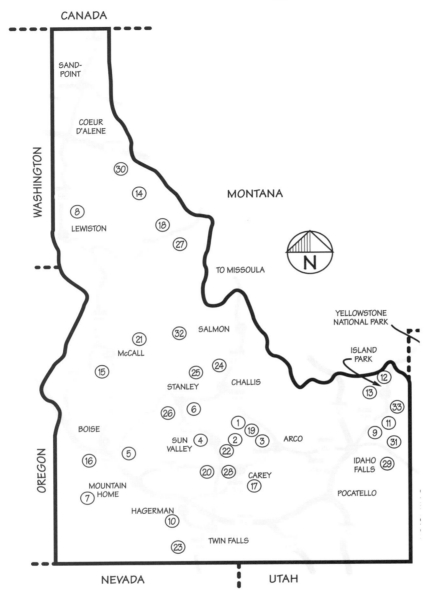

Profiled Streams, Lakes, and Reservoirs

1. Big Lost River
2. Big Lost River, East Fork
3. Big Lost River, Lower
4. Big Wood River
5. Boise River, South Fork
6. Boulder/White Cloud Peaks Area Lakes
7. C.J. Strike Reservoir
8. Clearwater River
9. Falls River
10. Hagerman Area

11. Henrys Fork
12. Henrys Lake
13. Island Park Reservoir
14. Kelly Creek
15. Lake Cascade
16. Lake Lowell
17. Little Wood River
18. Lochsa River
19. Mackay Reservoir
20. Magic Reservoir
21. Pinnacle Peak Area Lakes

22. Pioneer Area Lakes
23. Salmon Falls Creek Reservoir
24. Salmon River, Main & Upper
25. Salmon River, Middle Fork
26. Sawtooth Area Lakes
27. Selway River
28. Silver Creek
29. Snake River, South Fork
30. St. Joe River
31. Teton River
32. Twin Peaks Area Lakes
33. Warm River/Robinson Creek

Conditions by Month
Idaho Fly Fishing

FEATURED WATERS
① REFERS TO NUMBERS ON VICINITY MAP
BEST GOOD FAIR C CLOSED
NF No Fishing   WD Weather Dependent

FEATURED WATERS	JANUARY	FEBRUARY	MARCH	APRIL	MAY	JUNE	JULY	AUGUST	SEPTEMBER	OCTOBER	NOVEMBER	DECEMBER
① ② ③ Big Lost River				C	C							
② Big Wood River				C	C	NF						WD
⑤ Boise River, South Fork				C	C							
⑥ Boulder/White Cloud Peaks Area Lakes	NF	NF	NF	NF	NF	NF					NF	NF
⑦ C.J. Strike Reservoir	WD	WD										WD
⑧ Clearwater River						NF	NF					
⑨ Falls River	WD	WD	WD	NF	NF							NF
⑩ Hagerman Area												
⑪ Henrys Fork												
⑫ Henrys Lake	C	C	C	C	C						C	C
⑬ Island Park Reservoir	NF	NF	NF	NF							NF	NF
⑭ Kelly Creek	NF	NF	NF	NF	NF					WD	NF	NF
⑮ Lake Cascade	NF	NF	NF	NF							WD	NF
⑯ Lake Lowell	WD											WD
⑰ Little Wood River											C	WD
⑱ Lochsa River					NF	NF						
⑲ Mackay Reservoir	NF	NF	NF	NF								NF
⑳ Magic Reservoir												WD
㉑ Pinnacle Peak Area Lakes	NF	NF	NF	NF	NF						NF	NF
㉒ Pioneer Area Lakes	NF	NF	NF	NF	NF						NF	NF
㉓ Salmon Falls Creek Reservoir	WD	WD	WD	WD								WD
㉔ Salmon River, Main & Upper	NF	NF	NF		NF	NF						NF
㉕ Salmon River, Middle Fork	NF	NF	NF	NF	NF						NF	WD
㉖ Sawtooth Area Lakes	NF	NF	NF	NF	NF						NF	NF
㉗ Selway River	NF	NF	NF	NF	NF	NF					NF	NF
㉘ Silver Creek				C	C							
㉙ Snake River, South Fork				C	C							
㉚ St. Joe River	C	C	C	C	C					C	C	C
㉛ Teton River	C	C	C	C	C	C						C
㉜ Twin Peaks Area Lakes	NF	NF	NF	NF	NF						NF	NF
㉝ Warm River/Robinson Creek	C	C	C	C	C							C

Fly Fishing in Idaho
Thoughts on Regulations, Fish, and Water

Although each fly fishing water in Idaho has its own particular set of blueprints that dictate how it functions, there are also some general characteristics (some manmade, others created by nature) that tell us where, when, and even how to approach most of the angling in Idaho.

Idaho and some other western states now lead most of the country in restrictive or catch and release regulations, something I did not think I would say or write in my lifetime. These regulations help ensure good populations of quality fish now and in the future. Filling a creel with fish depletes the resource, is unproductive and outdated, and is now recognized by many as a poor management practice.

Speaking of fish, years ago the dominant species of trout in Idaho was the cutthroat. By the turn of this century, rainbow and to a lesser degree brook trout were added to many fisheries. Later, because of poor water quality, fishing pressure, and general degradation, the brown trout was added to many waters, Today a major effort to retain the cutthroat in Idaho is underway. For fly fishers, "cutts," rainbows, and browns are the state's primary game fish.

As good as Idaho's regulations are, however, it's the water the fish inhabit that make all the great fly fishing work. Idaho fly fishing waters can be divided into two basic regions, north and south. Most (but not all!) of the best fishing is located in the southern half of the state. Northern waters generally lack the levels of alkalinity necessary to produce strong aquatic insect populations and, in turn, fast-growing and large fish. But believe me, you will find enjoyable fly fishing in northern Idaho. This guide will show you the best waters and when to fish them.

Idaho's water, in one form or another, comes from winter snowpack. When this snow melts in the spring and early summer, many rivers and streams become high, off color, and unfishable. Fly fishers making travel plans for Idaho should take this into consideration. Always seek stream or lake information from a local source or fly shop.

I maintain that one of Idaho's most precious resources is water. To satisfy the needs of the state's major economic interest (agriculture), much of this water has been harnessed by dams to provide power and irrigation for farmlands. These impoundments often dictate where and when we fish Idaho's storied rivers and lakes. I find Idaho's whole system of hydroelectric/irrigation projects a double-sided coin. One side of the coin is the fact that dams do a good job of controlling the runoff. These projects can provide very good early-season fishing on rivers that otherwise would be swollen with spring snowmelt. Henrys Fork is a good example. Stream damage from runoff is also minimized by the controlled releases.

The flip side of this coin is the need for irrigation water in the dry season. Outflow levels can either be high or go up and down like a yo-yo. Both can be detrimental to the fishing and, in some cases, to the angler. Wading can be difficult if not impossible, and a boat may be the only means of access. Not until the storage of next year's irrigation water begins do water levels become prime. Taking all this into consideration, fall fishing in Idaho can be nothing short of spectacular.

Approximately 68% of Idaho land is government owned. Access to water on most of this land is good. The 32% that is private property can present access issues for anglers. By Idaho law if a stream is navigable, which most are, the state owns not only that water, but also the streambed up to the mean high water mark. Therefore, once you have accessed the water—as long as you did not trespass—you are well within your rights to move about or float the waters unrestricted. Always secure appropriate permission from the landowners.

Idaho is one of the last frontiers for quality western-type angling in this country. Idaho Fish and Game is setting aside more and more quality water, and water users are managing the resource better. As a result, Idaho fly fishing will be not only maintained but improved for future generations. But we still need your help. Respect the water systems; your fellow anglers and the bounty that lives in Idaho's rivers, streams, lakes, and reservoirs. Releasing fish to be caught and enjoyed another day is still one of our best hopes. Won't you consider these guidelines when fly fishing in Idaho, or anywhere else for that matter?

Abide by the laws.
Practice catch and release.
Respect property rights.
Carry out your litter.
Never crowd in on another fisher.

Idaho Fly Fishing Guidelines

I must make two points before I mention some general guidelines that relate to this guide. First, I've been totally honest about each body of water in this guide. If my experience is limited or when I relied on information from others, I've mentioned this. Second, because conditions change, keep in mind that this book is a guide, not the last word.

Information

No matter where you go fly fishing in Idaho, get information from people who regularly fish that area. Their knowledge, combined with the essential information here, can help you maximize your fly fishing experience. Many reliable sources of local information are listed in the back section of this guide. An area fly shop is your best spot for local information.

Regulations

In this guide I've noted some of Idaho's fishing regulations, especially the well-known ones that pertain to a particular water. But, because these regulations change from time to time, be sure always to check current state regulations before you head off fishing. The annual *Idaho General Fishing Seasons and Rules* is available at fly shops, sporting goods stores, and other outlets or from the Idaho Department of Fish and Game. I suggest you get a copy and review it. And don't forget a fishing license!

Hatches

It is not my intention to make this guide a "hatch book." But aquatic insects that are of interest to trout are one of my strong suits. Therefore, hatches that occur on some of the more popular fly fishing waters in Idaho are presented under the heading "Known Hatches." The important word here is *known*. Key hatches are presented in detailed hatch charts or given brief notice. When there is insufficient hatch information, the heading is eliminated. You can also infer some of the insect activity on a particular water based on the fly patterns listed under "Flies to Use" heading.

Words

This is a No Nonsense guide. I've tried to avoid a lot of small talk and extraneous detail and what the original No Nonsense author, Harry Teel (*Fly Fishing Central and Southeastern Oregon*) calls "unimportant falderal." I've provided essential and basic information that will help you select a fly fishing water in Idaho, and know what to take and what to expect. As a result you should, in a short amount of time, have a better chance of successfully fly fishing in Idaho.

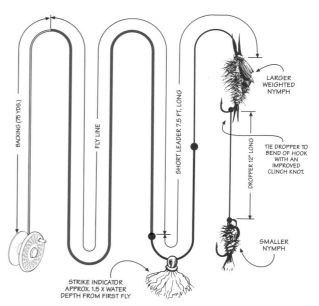

Using a large dry fly as a strike indicator can be very effective in Idaho. Use the dry fly as you would any strike indicator, except that it will hook a fish that rolls on it! Tie the dropper directly to the bend of the hook using an improved clinch knot.

Another popular two-fly rig for fly fishing in Idaho uses a typical strike indicator placed on the butt section of the leader roughly 1½ times the water depth from the first fly. Use a large weighted nymph as the first fly, then add a dropper and use a smaller nymph as a trailer.

Hatch Charts

S = Spinner Stage
D = Dun Stage
am = Sunrise to Noon
pm = Noon to 6 p.m.
eve = evening

Big Wood River Hatch Chart

HATCH	STAGE/TIME OF DAY	JAN	FEB	MAR	APR	MAY	JUN	JULY	AUG	SEPT	OCT	NOV	DEC
Drunella doddsi (green drake)	D, pm, S, all							█					
Epeorus longimanus (western quill Gordon)	D, pm							█	█				
Baetis sp. (blue-winged olive)	D, pm								█	█	█		
Epeorus deceptivus (cream dun)	D, pm—S, eve							█	█				
Heptagenia elegantula (pink dun)	D, pm—S, eve								█				
Rhithrogena hageni (western March brown)	D, pm								█	█			
Timpanoga hecuba (red quill)	D, pm									█			
Serratella tibialis (chocolate dun)	D, pm										█		
Stoneflies *Calineuria* (golden stone)	pm						█	█					
Isoperla, Isogenus sp. (small yellow stone)	pm						█	█					
Caddis *Hydropsyche* (spotted caddis)	pm, eve							█	█				
Oecetis (horned caddis)	pm, eve							█					
Colossosoma (tan caddis)	pm, eve							█					
Hydroptilidae (microcaddis)	pm, eve							█					
Midges	All Day	█	█	█		█		█			█	█	█

Silver Creek Hatch Chart

HATCH	STAGE/TIME OF DAY	JAN	FEB	MAR	APR	MAY	JUN	JULY	AUG	SEPT	OCT	NOV	DEC
Ephemera simulans (brown drake)	D, S, pm						█						
Ephemerella infrequens (pale morning dun)	S, am—D, pm						█	█	█				
Baetis parvus (*Diphetor hageni*) (little olive quill)	D, S, am						█	█	█	█			
Callibaetis sp. (speckled dun & spinner)	D, S, pm						█	█	█				
Tricorythodes minutus (trico)	S, am							█	█				
Ephemerella inermis (small pale morning dun)	D, pm								█				
Pseudocloen edmundsi (*planditus punctiventris*) (tiny blue-winged olive)	D, pm									█			
Baetis tricaudatus (blue-winged olive)	D, pm										█		
Paraleptophlebia debilis (slate-mahogany dun)	D, pm									█			
Caddis *Rhyacophila* (green caddis)	am						█						
Caddis *Brachycentrus* (tan caddis)	am & pm						█						
Midges (Sporadic)	All day	█	█	█			█					█	█

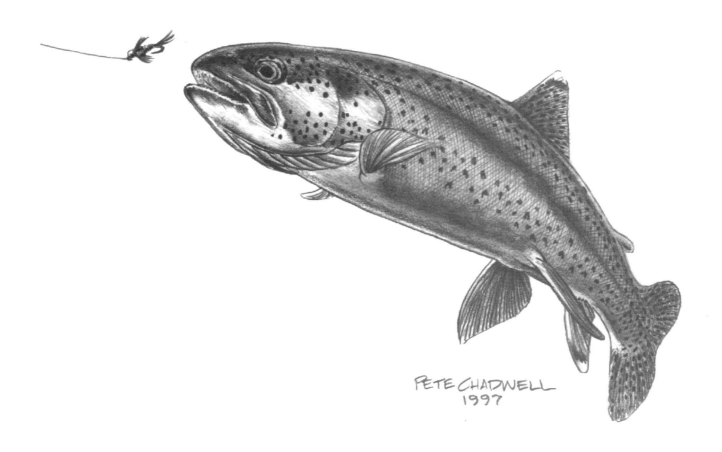

Rainbow Trout.

Common Game Fish in Idaho

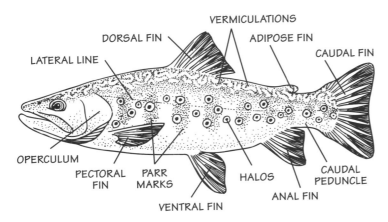

VERMICULATIONS
DORSAL FIN
ADIPOSE FIN
CAUDAL FIN
LATERAL LINE
OPERCULUM
PECTORAL FIN
PARR MARKS
VENTRAL FIN
HALOS
ANAL FIN
CAUDAL PEDUNCLE

Typical salmon, trout, or char. Most hatchery fish have a clipped adipose fin.

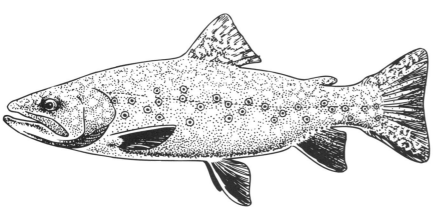

BROOK TROUT
"Brookies" are in the char family (Dolly, bull trout, lake trout, etc.). Back is black, blue-gray, or green with mottled, light-colored markings. Sides have red spots with blue rings. Tail is square. Lower fins are red, striped with black and white. Prefers colder water.

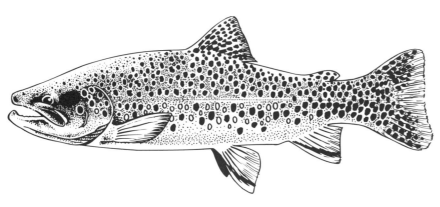

BROWN TROUT
The brown back has big black spots. The tail is square, and the sides have black and red spots with light blue rings. It's hard to catch and easily spooked.

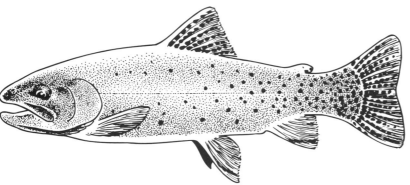

CUTTHROAT TROUT
Dark green back, flanks are golden to pink in color with black spots that increase in number towards the tail. The red jaw is the most telling marking.

Illustrations by Pete Chadwell. For fine art and fish renderings, contact: Dynamic Arts, 61858 Avonlea Circle, Bend, Oregon 97702. www.dynamicarts.com

MOUNTAIN WHITEFISH
Color is light brown or bronze to whitish; tail is split. Mouth is smaller than a trout's and doesn't extend back past the eye.

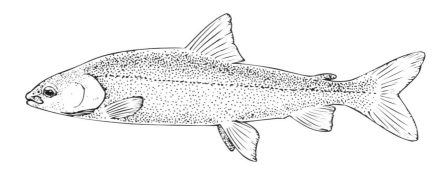

RAINBOW TROUT
The most abundant wild and hatchery fish. It has an olive-bluish back with small black spots. Each side has a light red or pink band. Lake 'bows are often all silver.

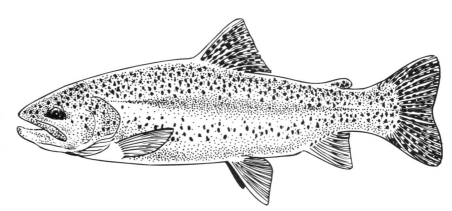

STEELHEAD TROUT
These trout leave rivers for the ocean and return to spawn several times. Similar to rainbows but with fewer spots; bigger and stronger. The tongue tip has teeth, but not the tongue back. Great fighting fish.

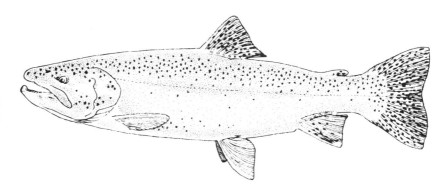

LARGEMOUTH BASS
Green back, silvery sides, large irregular spots. Deeply forked tail.

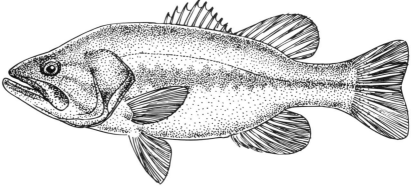

Best Flies to Use in Idaho

ADAMS

BEADHEAD PEACOCK STONE

BEADHEAD PHEASANT TAIL

BEADHEAD PRINCE

BLUE-WINGED OLIVE

DAVE'S HOPPER

DIVING CADDIS

ELK HAIR CADDIS

HARE'S EAR NYMPH

HUMPY

Illustrations by Pete Chadwell. For fine art and fish renderings, contact: Dynamic Arts, 61858 Avonlea Circle, Bend, Oregon 97702. www.dynamicarts.com

KAUFMAN'S STONE

MADAM X

PARACHUTE ADAMS

PMD COMPARADUN

PMD CRIPPLE

ROYAL WULFF

SCHROEDER'S PARA-HOPPER

SOFT HACKLE MIDGE

STIMULATOR

WOOLLY BUGGER

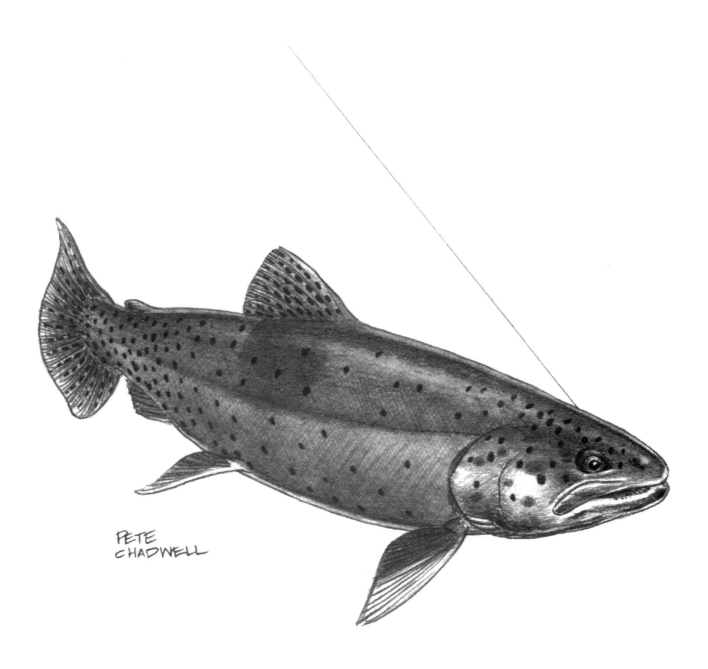

Cutthroat Trout.

Top Idaho
Fly Fishing Waters

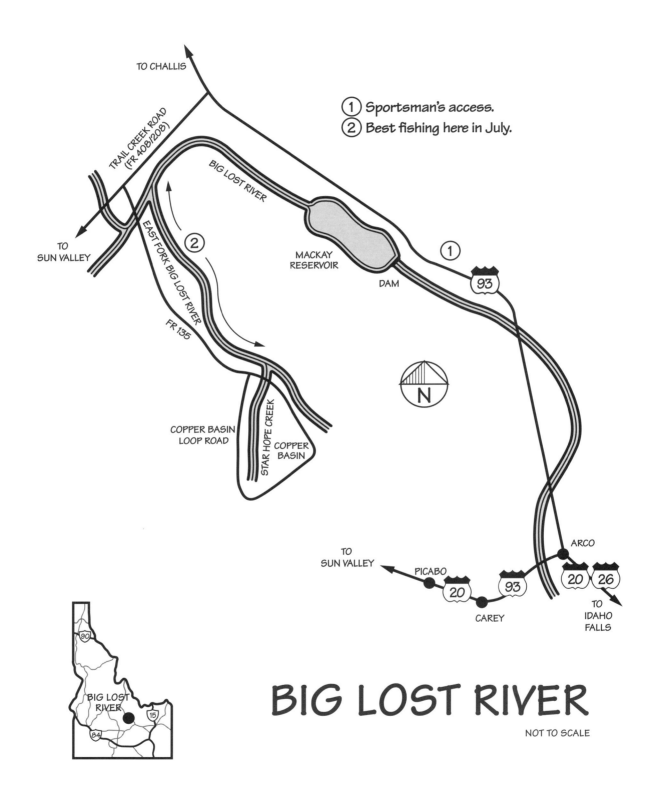

TO CHALLIS

① Sportsman's access.
② Best fishing here in July.

TRAIL CREEK ROAD (FR 408/208)

BIG LOST RIVER

TO SUN VALLEY

EAST FORK BIG LOST RIVER

②

MACKAY RESERVOIR

DAM

① 93

FR 135

N

COPPER BASIN LOOP ROAD

STAR HOPE CREEK

COPPER BASIN

ARCO

TO SUN VALLEY

PICABO

20

CAREY

93

20 26

TO IDAHO FALLS

90

BIG LOST RIVER

15

84

BIG LOST RIVER

NOT TO SCALE

Big Lost River

These rivers and headwaters are about 30 miles east of Sun Valley. They're some of the most fertile fly fishing water in the state and, depending on the time of year, can be the most productive "big fish" water in Idaho.

For the best fly fishing, head to the East Fork of the Big Lost in Copper Basin or to the Big Lost below Mackay Reservoir. The section from Mackay Reservoir upstream to the main river is beautiful water, but I'd avoid it. For a number of reasons, it has never been very productive.

East Fork: In the 1970s and 1980s, this section was great in July. Hatches were diverse and prolific. Now, unfortunately (despite fish limits) the fishery is a mere shadow of its former self. Check with fly shops in Sun Valley for conditions.

Lower Big Lost: When "on," this is great water for big fish. Hatches are infrequent but can produce sensational dry fly fishing. Nymphing is the most successful method here, even during hatches when fish seem to prefer the nymph to the winged version. Water below the reservoir is unwadable most of the summer.

To reach these waters from Sun Valley or Ketchum, take Trail Creek Road (FR408) and turn right on East Fork Road (FR135) and Copper Basin Loop Road (FR138). For the lower Big Lost, continue on Trail Creek Road to Highway 93, turn south past Mackay Reservoir, and look for the access signs along the road. Take Highway 93 north to access the river from Arco and the southeast.

Types of Fish
Rainbow, cutthroat, and cut bow in the upper section and some brook trout in the East Fork.

Known Hatches
East Fork—*July:* Mayflies: green drake (*Drunella, doddsi*), western quill (*Epeorus longimanus*) cream dun (*Epeorus deceptivus*), pink dun (*Heptagenia, elegantula*), Caddis: spotted caddis (*Hydropsyche*), horned caddis (*Oecetis*), tan caddis (*Glossosoma*), micro caddis (*Hydroptila*). Stoneflies: golden stone (*Calineuria*), small yellow stone (Isoperla and Isogenus).

Lower Big Lost—*Mid-June to Mid-July:* Pale morning dun (*Ephemerella inermis*), small yellow stone (*Isoperla mormona*, I. *patricia*, or Mormon girl), golden stone (*Calineuria*). *July–mid-Sept:* Olive crane fly (*Tipulidae*), some caddis. *October:* Blue-winged olive (*Baetis tricaudatus*). *February–March:* Midges and nymphs.

Equipment to Use
Rods: 5 to 6 weight, 8-½' to 9'.
Reels: Palm or mechanical drag.
Line: Floating line to match rod weight.
Leaders: 4x to 6x, 9'.
Wading: Chest-high neoprene waders with felt-soled wading boots. Wet-wade the East Fork in low water and warm weather. Wading can be treacherous below Mackay Reservoir in high water.

Flies to Use
East Fork—*Dry Patterns:* Green & Mason Green Drake & Gray Wulff #10–12; Western & Mason Western Quill, Parachute Adams & Cul-de-Canard (CDC) Rusty Spinner #14; Yellow Stimulator, Golden Stone, Madam X, Yellow Elk Hair Caddis #8–16; Henryville Special, Hemingway, King's River, & Elk Hair Caddis #14–18. *Nymphs:* Prince (beadhead & regular) #10–14; Brown Flashback #10–16, Pheasant Tail #12–16.

Lower Big Lost—*Dry Patterns:* Parachute, Emerger, Floating Nymph Pale Morning Dun, Pheasant Tail Flashback #16–18, Yellow Stimulator #8–14; Golden Stone, & Madam X #8; Olive Cranefly, Mackay Special, & Olive Cranefly Larva #12–14; BWO Parachute & Parachute Adams #16–20. *Nymphs:* Prince #8–14, Brown Flashback #12–18, Beaded Green Caddis Larva & Pheasant Tail #14–18, Olive or Black Woolly Bugger #6–10, Black Girdle Bug #8–10.

When to Fish
East Fork— Late June and July.
Lower Big Lost—Best is late June and July, October, February, and March.

Nearby Fly Fishing
Star Hope (West Fork of Lost), North Fork, and Wildhorse Creek, depending on fish stocking.

Seasons & Limits
Most of this section is open year-round. No live bait. Only two cutthroat at least 16". Winter is whitefish only; all trout must be released. Check the Idaho Fish & Game regulations.

Accommodation & Services
Some campgrounds. Hotels, motels, and other services are available in Sun Valley, Ketchum, Arco, and Mackay.

Rating
February to March the lower section is a 10. Because the East Fork has become very inconsistent and high water limits fishing in the lower section most of the summer, the overall rating is a 7.

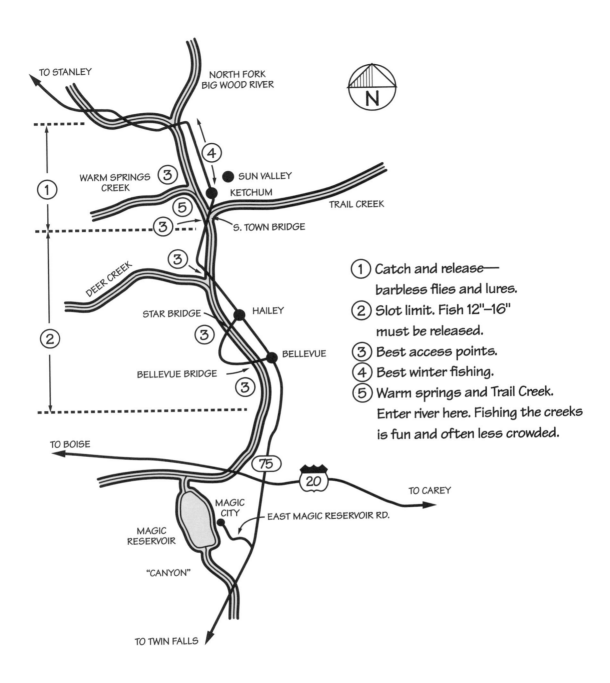

TO STANLEY

NORTH FORK
BIG WOOD RIVER

N

WARM SPRINGS
CREEK

③

④

● SUN VALLEY

KETCHUM

⑤

TRAIL CREEK

③ S. TOWN BRIDGE

DEER CREEK

③

STAR BRIDGE

③

● HAILEY

● BELLEVUE

BELLEVUE BRIDGE

③

TO BOISE

75

20

TO CAREY

MAGIC
CITY

EAST MAGIC RESERVOIR RD.

MAGIC
RESERVOIR

"CANYON"

TO TWIN FALLS

① Catch and release—
    barbless flies and lures.
② Slot limit. Fish 12"–16"
    must be released.
③ Best access points.
④ Best winter fishing.
⑤ Warm springs and Trail Creek.
    Enter river here. Fishing the creeks
    is fun and often less crowded.

BIG WOOD RIVER

NOT TO SCALE

Big Wood River

A rich, freestone-type stream, the Big Wood River flows through the Wood River Valley in the Ketchum/ Sun Valley area. Trout of high quality and good size challenge fly fishers most of the entire 75 miles of the Wood.

The most popular fishing area is from the town of Bellevue north to the North Fork of the Big Wood River. The section below Magic Reservoir, or "The Canyon," is good yet mystifying. Fall irrigation storage reduces the water flow to a mere trickle but surprisingly, heavy fish kills do not result.

The Big Wood can be accessed from many points off Highway 75 between Sun Valley (north) and Bellevue (south). Access to "The Canyon" is off Highway 75 on the road to Magic Dam. Much of the river is bordered with private property, which limits entry. Always check at a fly shop for public access or ask permission of landowners. Once on the river, travel below the high water mark is unrestricted.

Types of Fish
Rainbow trout.

Known Hatches (see hatch chart page 14)
Early July: Green drake (*Drunella*), Western quill Gordon (*Epeorus*), golden stone (*Calineuria*), small yellow stone (*Isoperla*).
July–August: Spotted caddis (*Hydropsyche*), horned caddis (*Oecetis*), tan caddis (*Glossosoma*), micro caddis (*Hydroptila*), cream dun (*Epeorus*), pink dun (*Heptagenia*).
July–October: Blue-winged olive (*Baetis*).
August–September: Western March brown (*Rithrogena*), red quill Gordon (*Timpanoga*).
September–October: Chocolate dun (*Serratella*).

Equipment to Use
Rods: 5 to 6 weight, 8½' to 9'.
Reels: Palm drag.
Lines: Floating lines matched to rod weight.
Leaders: 4x to 7x, 9' to 12'.
Wading: In low water during warm weather, wading shoes and shorts are fine. In high water use chest-high neoprene waders and felt-soled shoes for greater maneuverability.

Flies to Use (See Hatch Chart page 14)
General Use—*Dry Patterns:* Parachute Adams #12–22, Olive or Yellow Stimulator #10–14, Golden Stone #8, Elk Hair or Henryville Special Caddis #14–18, Rusty Spinner #16–18. *Nymphs:* Beaded Prince, Hares Ear, & Brown Flashback #10–16; Black or Olive Woolly Bugger #8–12.
July—*Dry Patterns:* Green Drake #10–12, Mason Green Drake, Gray Wulff, & Western Quill Gordon #14; Parachute Adams, Mason Western Quill, & Cul-De-Canard (CDC) Rusty Spinner #16–18; Golden Stone or Henry's Fork Golden Stone #8; Madam X, Small Yellow Stone, & Yellow Elk Hair Caddis #12; Henryville Special, Hemingway, King's River Caddis, Elk Hair Caddis #14–18. *Nymphs:* Beaded and regular Flashback #10, Hare's Ear, Prince #10–14.

August—*Dry Patterns:* Blue-Winged Olive #22; Olive Parachute or Adams Parachute #18; Cream Dun #16, Parachute Pale Morning Dun, & Little Cahill #16; CDC Rusty Spinner #16–18; Pink Dun #16–14, Light Cahill Parachute, or Pink Albert #16; Western March Brown #14–16; Tan Parachute #14–16.
September—*Dry Patterns:* Great Red Quill #10–12; Mason Red Quill or Gray Wulff #10; BWO, Little Olive Parachute, & Little Chocolate Dun #16; Adams Parachute #10–12. *Nymphs:* Beaded Prince, Hare's Ear #12–16; Midge Pupa #16–18.
Winter—Add Parachute Adams #20, Beaded Prince or Hare's Ear #12–16; Brassies, and White Midge Pupa #18–20 to the September selection.

When to Fish
July through October the upper section near Sun Valley is excellent. Winter fishing here can be good. August through October is the best time to fish the lower section. Entering the Big Wood River in Ketchum are Trail and Warm Springs Creeks, which can provide some very fun fly fishing.

Seasons & Limits
Seasons, limits and catch and release regulations vary for different sections of the river. Consult the Idaho Fish & Game regulations.

Accommodations and Services
Sun Valley, a major international resort, and Ketchum have an endless offering of accommodations, food, and services at all price ranges. Camping is available at the Forest Service campground 10 miles north of Ketchum. RV hookups are available one mile south of Ketchum.

Rating
The Big Wood is a great trout stream, a solid 9.

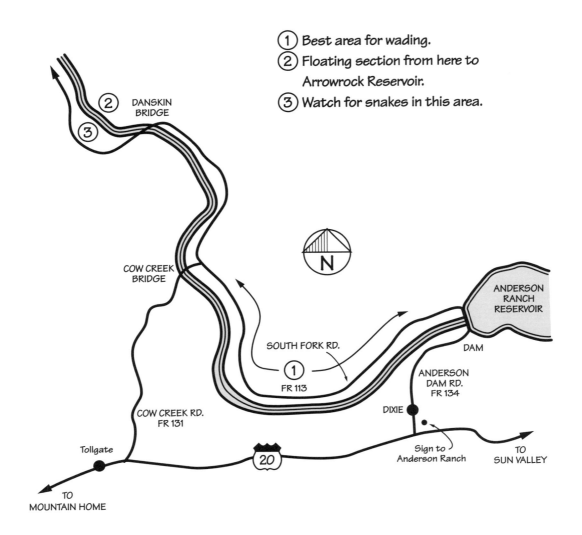

① Best area for wading.
② Floating section from here to Arrowrock Reservoir.
③ Watch for snakes in this area.

DANSKIN BRIDGE

ANDERSON RANCH RESERVOIR

N

COW CREEK BRIDGE

SOUTH FORK RD.

DAM

① FR 113

ANDERSON DAM RD. FR 134

COW CREEK RD. FR 131

DIXIE

Tollgate

20

Sign to Anderson Ranch

TO SUN VALLEY

TO MOUNTAIN HOME

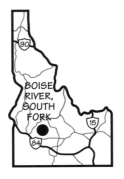

BOISE RIVER, SOUTH FORK

BOISE RIVER, SOUTH FORK

NOT TO SCALE

Boise River, South Fork

Residents of central and southwestern Idaho are fortunate to be very close to one of the state's best trout streams. It's not uncommon for businesspeople from Boise to leave work and, in about an hour, get into some great fly fishing.

The South Fork of the Boise, located east of Boise and north of Mountain Home, is a medium-sized freestone stream of high alkalinity and diverse and heavy aquatic insect populations. The upper section flowing into the reservoir has small trout and is not often fished. The major fly fishing action is on the two main sections below Anderson Ranch Dam.

The first section, 12 miles below the dam, is a picturesque river canyon that is easily accessed by road, and hence, often fished. Most of the 30 miles of the second section below Danskin Bridge is accessible only by boat or raft. This part of the river, called "rattlesnake gulch" by locals, demands a cautious eye for snakes. The river requires skilled boating techniques.

The quick route to the river is out of Mountain Home. Go 20 miles north on Highway 20, where you'll see signs announcing "Anderson Ranch Dam" and Dixie. Take Dixie Forest Road 134 downhill to the dam crossing, where river access begins. Downstream about 10 miles is Cow Creek Bridge, where a good dirt road provides access and entry to and from the river and connections to Highway 20.

Type of Fish
Wild rainbow trout.

Known Hatches
Mayflies
August–September: Blue-winged olive (*Baetis bicaudatus*), Pink Alberts (*Epeorus albertae*).
September–October: Blue-winged olive (*Baetis tricaudatus*).

Stoneflies
July–August: Little yellow stone (*Isoperla, Isogenus*), lime sally (*Alloperla*).
March: Early brown stone (*Brachyptera*).

Equipment to Use
Rods: 5 to 6 weight, 8½' to 9½'.
Reels: Mechanical or palm drag.
Lines: Floating lines matched to rod weight.
Leaders: 4x to 7x, 9' to 12'.
Wading: In low water, use chest-high neoprene waders and felt-soled shoes. In high water, use chest-high neoprene waders and felt-soled shoes, stream cleats, and a wading staff.

Flies to Use
Dry Patterns: (High water) Olive/Tan Elk Hair, Hemingway, & Goddard Caddis #12–16. (low water) Partridge, Black, or Brown King's River #14–18; Soft Hackle patterns in the pupa stage; Little Yellow Stone, Lime Sally, Early Brown Stone, & Yellow Partridge #12–16. Blue-Winged Olive #20; Pink Albert, Slate/Tan No-Hackle #14–16.

When to Fish
Around Labor Day, when water storage for the following year begins, the river level drops and the fabulous fly fishing begins. Most of the best fishing is from the dam to Cow Creek Bridge. The Cow Creek to Danskin stretch is also good.

Seasons & Limits
Artificial flies and lures, barbless hooks, two-trout limit under 20". During winter whitefish season, December 1 to March 31, trout must be released. See the Idaho Fish & Game regulations for updated seasons and limits.

Accommodations & Services
Limited campsites are available at Anderson Ranch Reservoir. Many motels and services in the city of Mountain Home.

Rating
In high water, a 7; in low water the rating quickly jumps to a 9.5.

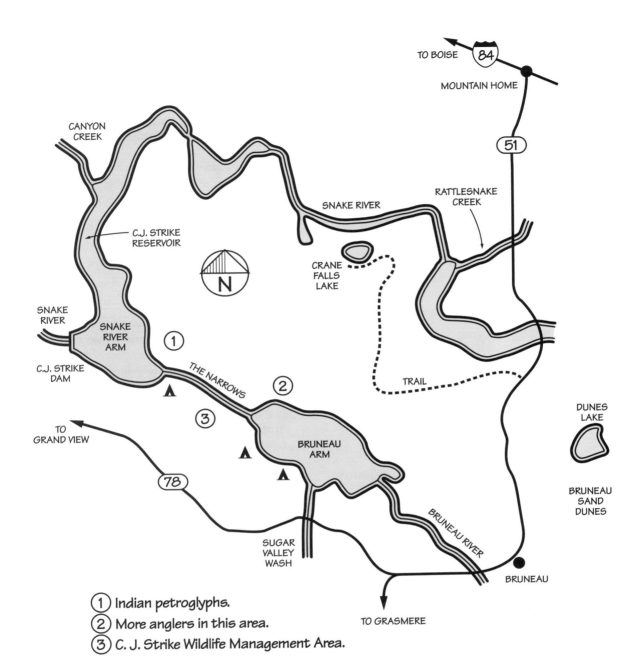

① Indian petroglyphs.
② More anglers in this area.
③ C. J. Strike Wildlife Management Area.

C.J. STRIKE RESERVOIR

NOT TO SCALE

C. J. Strike Reservoir

Idaho has a great alternative to, or respite from, fly fishing for trout: warmwater fish in ponds, pothole desert lakes, and even the lower sections of major rivers like the St. Joe and Snake. Plus, fly fishing for bluegill, crappie, and bass is generally best when either the trout season is closed or most waters are unfishable.

C. J. Strike Reservoir and the Bruneau area, the so called Desert Fishing Oasis are two of the best places for panfish and bass in the state. Located 20 miles southwest of Mountain Home (from Interstate 84 take Highway 51 south toward Bruneau), C. J. Strike is composed of two reservoirs, the Snake River arm and the Bruneau arm. There are more and larger bass in the Snake River section, but the insistent spring winds can be bothersome. The Bruneau arm, which consists of "The Narrows" and the upper deep section, has a good supply of fish but tends to have more anglers. Nearby Crane Falls Lake also provides excellent fishing.

Types of Fish

Abundant populations of bass, bluegill, crappie, and perch. There are also trout, though they're tough to find when the water is warm.

Equipment to Use

Bluegill, Crappie, Perch
Rods: 3 and 4 weight, 8' to 9'.
Reels: Palm drag.
Lines: Floating and sometimes sink tip.
Leaders: 4x and 5x, 9' to 12'.
Wading: Bank fishing or wading is ok with chest-high waders and felt-soled wading boots. It's best to fish from a boat or float tube.

Bass
Rods: 6 and 7 weight, 8' to 9½'.
Reels: Mechanical drag or single action type.
Lines: Floating and sometimes sink tip.
Leaders: 4x and 5x, 9' to 12'.
Wading: Bank fishing or wading is ok with chest-high waders and felt-soled wading boots. It's best to fish from a boat or float tube.

Flies to Use

Bluegill, Crappie, Perch
Subsurface: Brown Ostrich Leech, Marabou Nymph, small Leeches, small Lead Head Jigs, small Girdle Bug in black, brown, bright olive, chartreuse, & yellow #8–10.
Surface: Foam Spider, Cricket, small Popping Bugs in black, green, yellow, & white #10–12 (#8–10 for crappie).

Bass
Subsurface: Flashabou Woolly Bugger, beaded eyes or regular, in a variety of colors. Streamer patterns imitating chubs, yellow, black perch imitation tied Matuka style.
Surface: Poppers in many colors.

Tips: For subsurface fishing use a steady retrieve at various speeds. Cast poppers at target, then "pop" the bug by sharply snapping the rod back once. While the popper is resting on the surface, wiggle the rod back and forth to make it quiver.

When to Fish

Overall, May through mid-June tends to be most productive, as spawning activity is at its peak. Water temperatures should be in the low 60s for good success. Fish shallow areas along banks, outcroppings, other structure, flooded willows, weeds, and grasses, as well as small incoming streams. Also look for whitish areas near the shoreline indicating spawning beds. From September through November bass are loading up before winter and will strike readily, and trout are up closer to the surface.

Seasons & Limits

C. J. Strike can be fished year-round. Consult the Idaho Fish & Game regulations for any changes or limits. Currently there is a mercury contamination advisory for the reservoir.

Accommodations & Services

You can stay in Mountain Home, but it's easier to camp at the campgrounds at either reservoir. Black Sands Resort on the south shore of the Snake arm also has lodging. Near the dam on the north shore are displays of prehistoric Indian petroglyphs. An interesting side trip is to nearby Bruneau Dunes State Park and Dunes Lake. This water, now pumped from the Snake River, probably has more bluegill and bass than C.J. Strike Reservoir!

Rating

When conditions and water temperature are right, a 7.

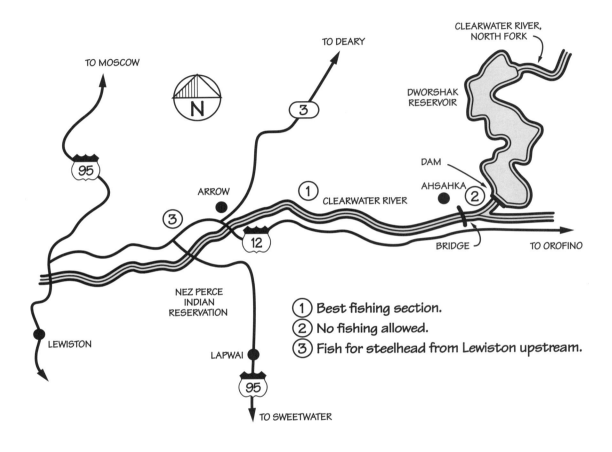

TO MOSCOW

TO DEARY

N

CLEARWATER RIVER,
NORTH FORK

DWORSHAK
RESERVOIR

95

3

DAM

AHSAHKA

3

ARROW

1 CLEARWATER RIVER

2

95

12

BRIDGE

TO OROFINO

NEZ PERCE
INDIAN
RESERVATION

1 Best fishing section.
2 No fishing allowed.
3 Fish for steelhead from Lewiston upstream.

LEWISTON

LAPWAI

95

TO SWEETWATER

CLEARWATER RIVER

NOT TO SCALE

Clearwater River

The Clearwater has long been considered Idaho's top steelhead river, boasting a strain of these fish that can exceed 20 pounds. These "B" run fish (versus the smaller "A" run) enter the Columbia River on August 25 after spending two or three years in the ocean. They return as brutes in good condition and are much more active than the steelhead that remain over the winter months and are fished in the spring. Look for steelhead in the lower third of pools and runs especially above heavy riffles and whitewater.

Clearwater River trout populations tend to be slim or limited. But if trout is your game, you will find some cutthroat and steelhead smolts.

Types of Fish
Primarily steelhead and smolts with some cutthroat and bass in the lower sections.

Equipment to Use
Steelhead
Rods: 8 or 9 weight, 9'.
Reels: Mechanical drag is best, palm drag will work.
Line: Floating or sink tip to match rod weight.
Leaders: 0x or 1x, 7' to 9'.
Wading: Use chest-high neoprene waders with felt-soled wading shoes.

Trout
Rods: 5 to 6 weight, 7½' to 9'.
Reels: Palm drag.
Lines: Floating lines matched to rod weight.
Leaders: 4x to 7x, 9' to 12'.
Wading: Use chest-high neoprene waders with felt-soled boots.

Flies to Use
Steelhead—Green Butted Skunk, Thor, Skykomish Sunrise, Purple Peril, Giant Fall Orange Caddis (wet) and Bucktail Caddis (dry) #4–8. The Bomber series, large Royal Wulff, and Grasshopper, skated and twitched on the swing, will work. Atlantic salmon Spey-type patterns are also being used here with success.

Trout—*Dry Patterns:* Royal Wulff, Elk Hair Caddis, Adams, Parachute Adams, & Golden Stone #8; Yellow Stimulator #6–8. *Nymphs:* Prince, Hares Ear, & Brown Stonefly #10–14.

When to Fish
The best steelhead fishing occurs during the catch and release period August 1 to October 15. Most is done from the city of Lewiston upstream, to Ahsahka Bridge, just downstream of Dworshak Dam. After October 15 it's "catch & keep". Fish for trout all season.

Seasons & Limits
Idaho's steelhead waters have special regulations, seasons, and boundaries. Consult the Idaho Fish & Game regulations. Open year-round for trout; barbless hooks only.

Accommodations & Services
The cities of Lewiston and Orofino have everything you need.

Rating
If the steelhead run is good an 8, if not, a 3.

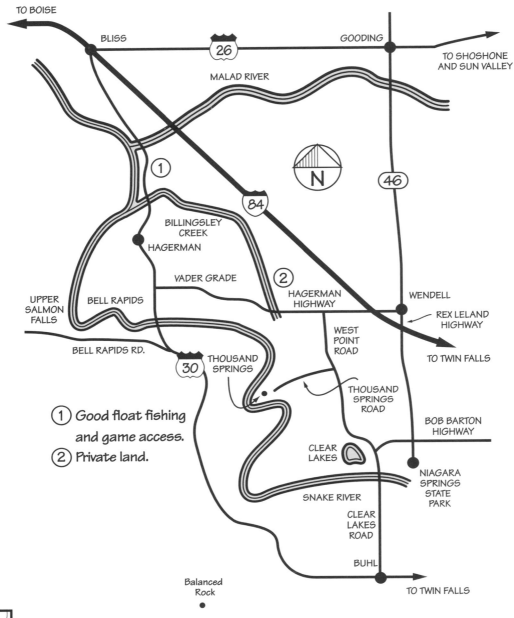

TO BOISE

BLISS

26 US

GOODING

TO SHOSHONE
AND SUN VALLEY

MALAD RIVER

1

84

46

N

BILLINGSLEY
CREEK

HAGERMAN

VADER GRADE

2

HAGERMAN
HIGHWAY

WENDELL

REX LELAND
HIGHWAY

UPPER
SALMON
FALLS

BELL RAPIDS

WEST
POINT
ROAD

TO TWIN FALLS

BELL RAPIDS RD.

30

THOUSAND
SPRINGS

THOUSAND
SPRINGS
ROAD

① Good float fishing
and game access.
② Private land.

BOB BARTON
HIGHWAY

CLEAR
LAKES

NIAGARA
SPRINGS
STATE
PARK

SNAKE RIVER

CLEAR
LAKES
ROAD

BUHL

Balanced
Rock

TO TWIN FALLS

HAGERMAN AREA

NOT TO SCALE

Hagerman Area

Fishing in Idaho during April, May, and early June can be limited by area closures or unfavorable water conditions. The Hagerman area presents a unique water situation that solves this seasonal dilemma.

Located in the south central part of the state, this area is fed by five major river systems and an aquifer located beneath the upper Snake River plain. After some 4,000 years underground, water gushes forth (in many places) through the walls of the Snake River Canyon between Twin Falls and Hagerman. This pure water is used to produce 95% of the commercially raised trout in the United States. The water in Niagara Springs, Thousand Springs, Clear Lakes, Billingsley Creek, and the Bell Rapids area on the Snake River provide some very good fly fishing.

These springs contain a fair number of trout, given their relatively short run into the Snake River. In some stretches the spring water is almost too pure, and aquatic insect populations suffer. Trout rarely grow over 16 inches in this water. In areas that are not entirely spring-fed, larger trout can be found.

The toughest part about fishing this area is finding the waters. Traveling the farm roads of southern Idaho is not always easy. These directions will get you as close as any. Use Wendell as a starting point and, if all else fails, ask for directions in Simerly's general store in Wendell.

Thousand Springs/Clear Lake—Take Hagerman Highway and turn left on West Point Road (some call it Clear Lakes Road) and go about 4 miles. Before dropping into the Snake River Canyon, turn right at Thousand Springs Road. For Clear Lakes, continue on West Point into the canyon. Clear Lakes is at the canyon base.

Billingsley Creek—Take the main road to Hagerman. At the base of Vader Grade cross Billingsley Creek, where access is limited. Or, travel west on Highway 30 from the town of Hagerman. Check in Wendell for access to lower Billingsley.

Bell Rapids—Take Hagerman Highway to U.S. Route 30, east of the town of Hagerman. Turn left toward Buhl and go over the bridge crossing the Snake River. Fish downstream of the bridge.

Niagara Springs—Take Rex Leland Highway (the main road) south out of Wendell. Follow the road into the base of Snake River Canyon and look for Niagara.

Types of Fish
Rainbow and a few browns in the Snake River.

Known Hatches
April–May: Blue-winged olives (*Baetis*).
June–July: Pale morning dun (*Ephemerella inermis*).

Equipment to Use
Rods: 4 to 6 weight, 8½' to 9'.
Reels: Click drag, single action.
Lines: Floating and sink tip lines matched to rod weight.
Leaders: 4x to 7x, 9' to 12'.
Wading: Water is very cold, use chest-high neoprene waders and felt-soled shoes. In the Bell Rapids area above upper Salmon Falls and Clear Lakes use a float tube or boat.

Flies to Use
Spring Creeks—*Dry Patterns:* Baetis #18–22; Brown Caddis #16; Parachute Adams & Olive Dun #18–20; Parachute Pale Morning Dun #16–20; King's River and Partridge Caddis #14–18. *Nymphs:* Pheasant Tail, Brown Flashback #14–18.

Bell Rapids—*Wet Patterns:* Black, Black/Olive, and variegated Brown Woolly Buggers #2–8.
Clear Lakes—*Wet Patterns:* Green Damsel, Black/Brown Marabou Leech, & Staynor Ducktail #6–10, Freshwater Shrimp #10–12.

When to Fish
Fish the springs and creeks and Bell Rapids in the early spring. Try Clear Lakes in the spring and fall.

Seasons & Limits
Many of these waters have special regulations. Consult the Idaho Fish & Game regulations booklet for complete area information.

Accommodations & Services
Find motels in Wendell and Buhl, restaurants in Hagerman.

Rating
If the spring creeks had bigger fish, the rating would be quite high. As it is, a 6.5.

Henrys Fork of the Snake River Hatch Chart

SECTION	HATCH	STAGE/ TIME OF DAY	FEB	MAR	APR	MAY	JUN	JULY	AUG	SEPT	OCT	NOV
1, 2, 4, 5	*Baetis* sp. (blue-winged olive)	D, pm	■	■								
1, 2, 5	*Ephemerella inermis* (small pale morning dun)	S, am / D, am-pm					■	■				
1, 2, 5	*Drunella* (formerly *Ephemerella*) *grandis grandis* (green drake)	D, pm					■					
1, 2	*Ephemera simulans* (brown drake)	D, S, eve					■					
5	*Siphlonurus occidentalis* (gray drake)	S, eve								■		
1, 2, 5	*Drunella* (formerly *Ephemerella*) *flavilinea* (leadwing olive)	D, pm / S, eve						■				
1, 2	*Pseudocloen edmundsi* (*Plauditus puntiventris*) (tiny blue-winged olive)	D, pm							■			
1	*Tricorythodes minutus* (trico)	S, am							■			
1	*Callibaetis nigritus* (speckled spinner)	S, am							■			
1, 2, 5	*Paraleptophlebia bicornuta* (slate-mahogany dun)	D, pm									■	
1, 2, 5	*Baetis tricaudatus* (blue-winged olive)	D, pm									■	
3, 4, 5, 6	Stoneflies *Pteronarcys* sp. (salmonfly)	pm				■	■					
3, 4, 6	*Acrineuria* sp. (golden stone)	pm						■				
3, 4, 6	*Isogenus* sp. (small yellow stone)	pm						■	■			
2, 3, 4, 5, 6	*Caddis* spp. Various sp.	all day			■		■	■				

KEY

1. Harriman State Park
2. Osborne/Riverside
3. Riverside/Warm River
4. Warm River/Ashton
5. Chester (Sealy's farm)
6. Box Canyon

S = Spinner Stage
D = Dun Stage
am = Sunrise to Noon
pm = Noon to 6 p.m.
eve = evening

Henrys Fork of the Snake River

In the last 20 years the notoriety of Henrys Fork has reached every corner of the fly fishing world. Located in the upper northeast part of Idaho, "The Fork" provides some 50 miles of the most complex river fly fishing in the West. Highways 20 and 191 leading to Yellowstone National Park is the main corridor.

This river will always have a very special place in my heart. It was on this river some 25 years ago that I started, learned, and applied my professional career. In these early years, with the river almost to myself, I helped discover insect hatches and develop many fly patterns for "The Fork." Ah, for those times again.

Probably the peak fly fishing years on "The Fork" were from 1970 to the mid-1980s. In the late '80s a sharp decline in fish populations occurred. Mike Lawson, owner of Henry's Fork Anglers and present "Dean" of Henrys Fork explained, "Many complex and interrelated reasons led to the river's recent decline. A recent study showed that during the drought years, siltation occurred, hurting spawning and fry habitat. Normally, this is flushed out in the spring, but because water was stored in Island Park Reservoir during the drought years (1987–1992), this did not happen. This knowledge and better cooperation among government agencies, means we believe we can restore 'The Fork' to its former glory." Present challenges aside, Henrys Fork is one of the great and classic dry fly streams in the world.

Because it is easier to understand this complicated river section by section, I will depart slightly from the standard No Nonsense format. The basic information needed to fly fish all sections of Henrys Fork is summarized below. The pages that follow describe each section, starting upstream and moving downstream.

Types of Fish

Primarily rainbow trout with a decent population of brown trout in the lower river from Warm River downstream. Some brook trout can be found in Box Canyon and the upper river.

Known Hatches

The extensive hatches of Henrys Fork are presented in the hatch chart on the facing page. Refer to this chart for each of the river sections that follow.

Equipment to Use

Rods: For flat, smooth water, 3 to 6 weight, 8' to 9'. For casting big dry flies, 6 to 7 weight, 8½' to 9½'. For big weighted nymphs and streamers, 7 to 8 weight, 9' to 9½'.

Reels: Mechanical or palm drag.

Lines: Floating lines to match rod weight.

Leaders: 4x and 5x, 9' for dry flies. 4x, 7' to 9' with split shot weights and a strike indicator for nymphing.

Wading: Use chest-high neoprene waders with felt-soled shoes. A boat or raft is helpful in most sections. If you are unfamiliar with this section of river or boating in general, consult a qualified guide or outfitter before taking to the river in a boat.

Accommodations & Services

There are small motels in St. Anthony and Ashton. Most people stay in the Last Chance/Island Park area. Camping is available in Forest Service areas, primarily at Box Canyon. Cabins can be rented at Pond's Lodge and Mack's Inn. Alpenhaus Motel in Last Chance is also convenient. RV hookups at the KOA, Ponds Lodge and McCreas Ranch (off Shotgun Valley Road). Up-scale accommodations (food included) can be found at Elk Creek Ranch, Henry's Fork Lodge, and Three Rivers Ranch at Warm River. Restaurants, groceries, and gas are readily available.

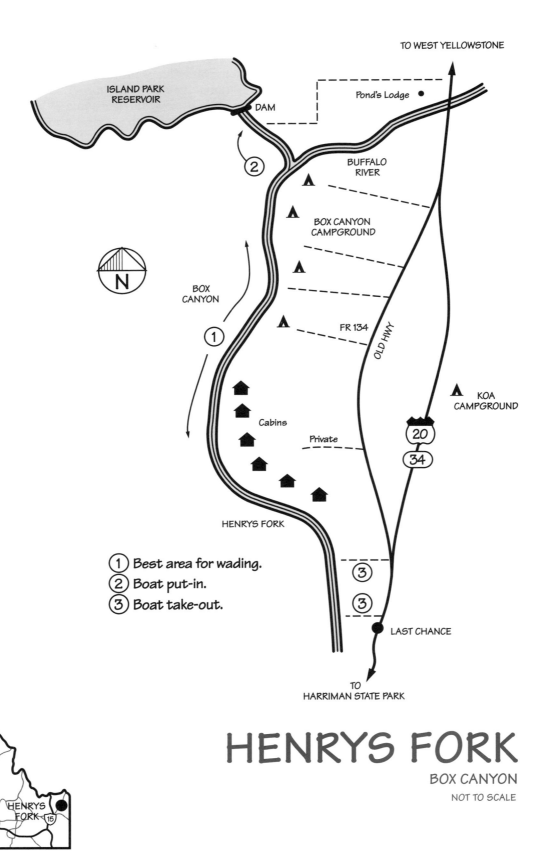

TO WEST YELLOWSTONE

ISLAND PARK
RESERVOIR

Pond's Lodge

DAM

②

BUFFALO
RIVER

N

BOX
CANYON

BOX CANYON
CAMPGROUND

①

FR 134

OLD HWY

Cabins

KOA
CAMPGROUND

Private

20

34

HENRYS FORK

① Best area for wading.
② Boat put-in.
③ Boat take-out.

③

③

LAST CHANCE

TO
HARRIMAN STATE PARK

HENRYS FORK

BOX CANYON

NOT TO SCALE

HENRYS
FORK

Henrys Fork Box Canyon

Quite simply, this canyon, below Island Park Dam is quite simply a gorgeous place to cast a fly. Truly monster trout patrol this three-mile stretch, and their presence has enticed fly fishers for years. In this section, one has a reasonable opportunity to take a 10-pound trout on a dry fly, big nymph, or streamer, but it's a challenge. This area has fast water, odd-shaped boulders and slick rocks, making wading difficult. For this reason many anglers don't fish "The Canyon."

If you are wading this section, take Forest Road 134 from Last Chance. Various dirt roads, including Box Canyon Campground Road, leading off it take you to the canyon rim. If floating, the put-in is below Island Park Dam and the take-out is at Last Chance.

Types of Fish
Mostly rainbows with some brook trout.

Known Hatches
Box Canyon is paved with mayflies, caddisflies, and small stoneflies. Because of the fast, turbulent water, precise imitations are not necessary. For the salmonfly hatch, fish the lower and middle sections in early June, and fish the upper section in mid-June. The golden stone hatch usually occurs between June 20 and July 15.

Flies to Use
Dry Patterns: Royal Wulff, Humpy, & Elk Hair Caddis #14–16; Stimulator #10–14.
Nymphs: Prince #8–12, Flashback, Hare's Ear #10–14.
Salmonfly hatch: Salmon Fly #4–6, Henry's Fork & Bird's Salmon Fly #4–6, Black Rubber Leg Nymph #2–4.
Golden Stone Hatch: Golden stone & Salmon Fly tied in Golden Stone colors #6–8, Black Rubber Leg #4–8, Sculpin-type streamers #2–4.

When to Fish
Fish all season for trout in the 8" to 14" range. For larger trout, fish from June to July 10 and from September 20 through October, casting heavily weighted nymphs and sculpin-type streamers. The short-lived salmonfly and golden stone hatches in June and early July is an excellent time for big fish.

Seasons & Limits
General season; catch and release only with artificial lures and barbless hooks; no boat motors. Seasons and limits can change, consult the Idaho Fish & Game regulations.

Rating
In June with the salmonfly hatch, a 9. Overall a 6.

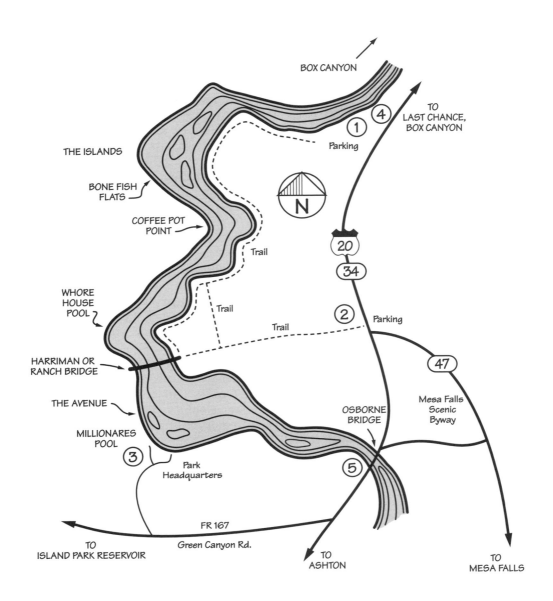

BOX CANYON

THE ISLANDS

BONE FISH
FLATS

COFFEE POT
POINT

Trail

WHORE
HOUSE
POOL

Trail

Trail

HARRIMAN OR
RANCH BRIDGE

THE AVENUE

MILLIONARES
POOL

④ TO
LAST CHANCE,
BOX CANYON

① Parking

N

20

34

② Parking

47

Mesa Falls
Scenic
Byway

OSBORNE
BRIDGE

⑤

③ Park
Headquarters

FR 167

Green Canyon Rd.

TO
ISLAND PARK RESERVOIR

TO
ASHTON

TO
MESA FALLS

① Park, walk, and wade.
② Park and walk to river from here.
③ Leave car at Park Headquarters.
④ Boat put-in.
⑤ Boat take-out.

HENRYS FORK
HARRIMAN STATE PARK—RAILROAD RANCH
NOT TO SCALE

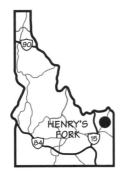

HENRY'S
FORK

Henrys Fork—Harriman State Park

To many fly fishers the seven miles of river in the Last Chance/Harriman State Park area is Henrys Fork. Despite siltation, weeds, and regulations, this is some of the greatest dry fly water in the United States. "The Ranch" (as many locals still call it) may be famous, but that doesn't mean it's easy to fly fish. Hatches present themselves readily yet don't always indicate what the fish are eating. And, as this area is a prolific aquatic insect factory, you are continually faced with complex hatch situations. At times as many as five species of mayflies, in various stages, can be on the water at the same time. Add simultaneous caddis activity and things get even more challenging.

To get to this fabled section of water, take Highway 20 north toward Last Chance and look for a turnoff and parking lot for the upper section. For the middle section, access the river from Middle Ranch Road where Highways 20 and 47 intersect. Park here and walk down to the river. To access the lower section, turn off Highway 20 at Green Canyon Road (near Osborne Bridge) and head for the park headquarters.

Walking and wading are the most common ways to fish this area. Floating is also popular on this section, because it provides convenient access to all the water. Boat put-in is at Last Chance near the north end of the park. Take-out is at Osborne Bridge.

Types of Fish
Rainbow trout.

Hatches & Flies to Use

June
Look for a dun hatch on June mornings and a spinner fall in the late mornings and evenings.
Dry Patterns: Pale Morning Dun #14–20; Gray/Yellow No-Hackle #16–20; Parachute Pale Morning Dun and Thorax #18; Western Green Drake #10, Green Drake Paradun, & Crippled Dun Drake #10.
Nymphs: Crippled Green Drake Dun & Brown Flashback #14–16.

July
The July *Drunella flavilinea* hatch is considered the best hatch on the Ranch section.
Dry Patterns: Flav's or Leadwing Olive #14; Western Slate Olive Dun, Slate/Olive No-Hackle & Olive Parachute #14–16; Brown Drake #10; Paradun Brown Drake, & Partridge Brown Drake Spinner, CDC Hen Rusty Spinner #14–16; Pale Morning Dun #20.

August
Mid-August brings a sporadic morning *Callibaetis* spinner fall. A huge *Baetis* hatch occurs late in the month.
Dry Patterns: Speckled Spinner, Partridge Spinner, Gray Parachute & Slate/Gray No-Hackle #14–16; Pale Olive Dun #20–22; Pale Olive Parachute #22; Trico or White/Black Spinner, White/Black Hen Spinner CDC #18–20; grasshoppers.

September
Paraleptophlebia emerges in afternoons from mid-September into October.
Dry Patterns: Slate Mahogany Dun #16, Slate/Tan or Slate Mahogany No-Hackles, Regular and Parachute Chocolate Duns #16; Fall Blue-Winged Olive #20; Gray/Light Olive No-Hackle or Parachute, slowwater Caddis #14–20.
Nymphs: Pheasant Tail & Mason Baetis #18.

Additional Notes: 5x tippets are often used here, although 6x is common and 7x is getting more popular. Try downstream, drag-free presentations, though some upstream casting can be successful. Caddis activity in this area (and in Last Chance) can be heavy, especially in June and July. Also try Terrestrials: Black Ant, Brown Flying Ant, and Black Beetle #14–18.

Seasons & Limits
Consult the Idaho Fish & Game regulations. Harriman State Park is open from June 15 to November 30; regulations are catch and release, barbless flies only. Below Harriman State Park the river is open year-round with a two-trout limit.

Rating
Years ago, as a classic dry fly stream this area was a 10. In the mid-1990s it dropped to a 5, but when this area "comes back" it will quickly return to a 10.

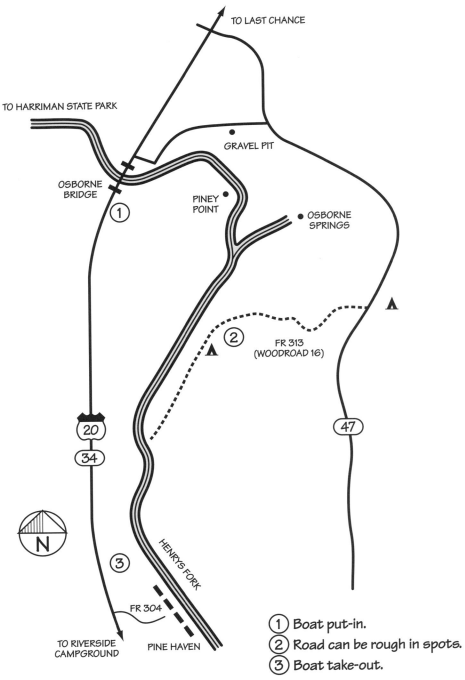

TO LAST CHANCE

TO HARRIMAN STATE PARK

GRAVEL PIT

OSBORNE
BRIDGE

①

PINEY
POINT

● OSBORNE
SPRINGS

FR 313
(WOODROAD 16)

②

20

34

N

47

③

HENRYS FORK

FR 304

TO RIVERSIDE
CAMPGROUND

PINE HAVEN

① Boat put-in.
② Road can be rough in spots.
③ Boat take-out.

HENRYS FORK
OSBORNE BRIDGE TO PINE HAVEN
NOT TO SCALE

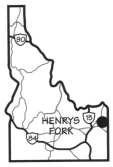

HENRYS
FORK

Henrys Fork
Osborne Bridge to Pine Haven

Over the years this area has been called the Gravel Pit, Osborne Springs, Piney Point or the most commonly accepted label, Woodroad 16. Though similar in structure to the nearby Harriman State Park section, the slow meandering river runs deep, so crossing is possible only at selected spots.

Easy and quick access add to the many positive attributes of this water. To get to the upper section, from Highway 20 go to Osborne Bridge, turn east (downstream) and follow a dirt road to the gravel pit road. Or take the Mesa Falls Scenic Byway (Highway 47) two or three miles to reach a dirt road marked Woodroad 16 that heads toward the river.

Woodroad 16 is a rough logging road that, especially when wet, can be an adventure requiring four wheel drive in some locations. If you float, put-in at Osborne Bridge, and take-out at Pine Haven, a private residential area.

Types of Fish
Rainbow trout.

Hatches & Flies to Use
June
Look for a dun hatch on June mornings and a spinner fall in the late mornings and evenings.
Dry Patterns: Pale Morning Dun #14–20; Gray/Yellow No-Hackle #16–20; Parachute Pale Morning Dun and Thorax #18; Western Green Drake #10; Green Drake Paradun #10; Crippled Dun Drake #10.
Nymphs: Crippled Dun Nymph.

July
Dry Patterns: Flav's or Leadwing Olive #14; Western Slate Olive Dun, Slate/Olive No-Hackle, and Olive Parachute #14–16; Brown Drake, Paradun Brown Drake, Partridge Brown Drake Spinner #10; CDC or Hen Rusty Spinner #14–16; Pale Morning Dun #20.

August
Mid-August brings a sporadic morning *Callibaetis* spinner fall. A huge *Baetis* hatch occurs late in the month.
Dry Patterns: Speckled Spinner #14–16; Partridge Spinner, Gray Parachute, & Slate/Gray No-Hackle #14–16; Pale Olive Dun #20–22; Pale Olive Parachute #22; Trico or White/Black Spinner, CDC, & White/Black Hen Spinner #18–20; Grasshoppers.

September
Paraleptophlebia emerges in the afternoons from mid-September into October.
Dry Patterns: Slate Mahogany Dun #16, Slate/Tan and Slate Mahogany No-Hackles, Regular and Parachute Chocolate Duns #16; Fall Blue-Winged Olive #20; Gray/light Slow Water Olive No-Hackle, & Parachute Caddis #14–20.
Nymphs: Pheasant Tail & Mason Baetis #18; Slow Water Caddis #14–20.
Terrestrials: Black Ant, Brown Flying Ant, Black Beetle, Grasshopper #14–18.

Seasons & Limits
General season, catch and release, artificial flies and lures only, no boat motors. Consult the Idaho Fish & Game regulations.

Rating
In June a solid 8, at other times this section slips to a 5.

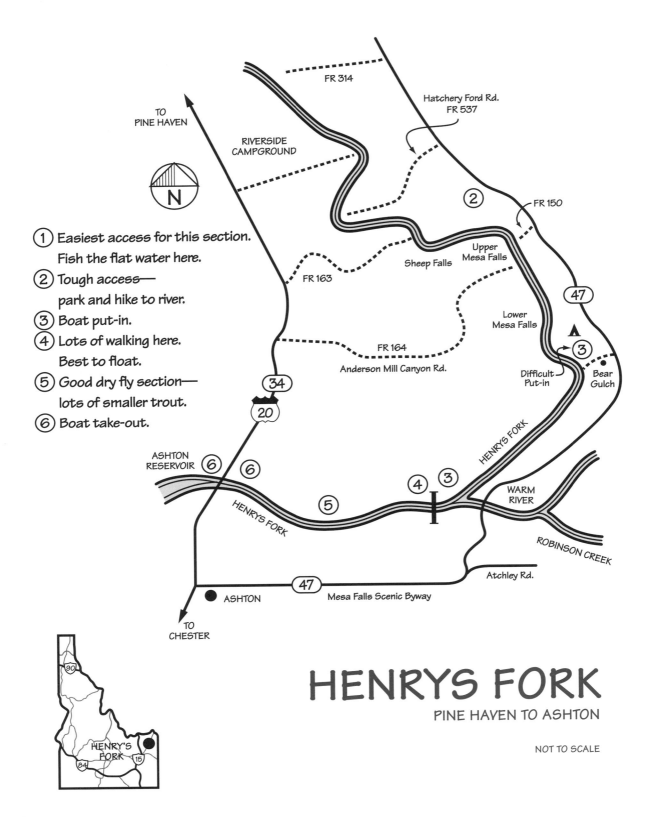

TO PINE HAVEN

N

RIVERSIDE CAMPGROUND

FR 314

Hatchery Ford Rd.
FR 537

FR 150

① Easiest access for this section. Fish the flat water here.

② Tough access—park and hike to river.

③ Boat put-in.

④ Lots of walking here. Best to float.

⑤ Good dry fly section—lots of smaller trout.

⑥ Boat take-out.

FR 163

Sheep Falls

Upper Mesa Falls

②

47

Lower Mesa Falls

③

Difficult Put-in

Bear Gulch

FR 164

Anderson Mill Canyon Rd.

34

20

ASHTON RESERVOIR

⑥

⑥

HENRYS FORK

⑤

④ ③

HENRY'S FORK

WARM RIVER

ROBINSON CREEK

Atchley Rd.

47

Mesa Falls Scenic Byway

ASHTON

TO CHESTER

HENRYS FORK

PINE HAVEN TO ASHTON

NOT TO SCALE

HENRY'S FORK

90

84   15

Henrys Fork–Pine Haven to Ashton

Pine Haven to Warm River—This remote area is highly rated for scenic beauty and is a good spot to get away from humans. However, you must work inordinately hard to get into fish on this water. Over the years I've floated the tricky whitewaters. I've four-wheeled into the canyon and descended carefully to fish all the remote sections. I've even dragged a boat down Bear Gulch and floated out. Yet despite these gargantuan efforts, I've not found enough quality fish here to justify all the hard work. The possible exception is the area upstream of Riverside Campground. Mayfly and caddis hatches on the flat water and a lingering salmonfly hatch make this area quite enjoyable. It's also more accessible.

From the Mesa Falls Scenic Byway (Highway 47) look for any number of forest roads that lead to the canyon. You'll have to park at the canyon rim and hike down to the river. Consult a topographical map and get more information from a local fly shop. If you do venture into the canyon, you probably won't find me crowding your space.

Warm River to Ashton—This is a very popular section of river to float. Considering the size of this water, big fish don't seem to surface feed here very much. The one exception is during the salmonfly hatch in early June. If fishing a dry fly and catching and releasing a boatload of fish from 8 to 12 inches (with an occasional 16 incher) is what you want, this section is for you.

From Island Park, take the Mesa Falls Scenic Byway (Highway 47) to Warm River. Take the dirt road that crosses Henrys Fork to the put-in. You can also reach this spot by taking the same highway east, through the town of Ashton.

This section can be waded, but river access is limited. You must walk a lot, either down the bank or along the railroad tracks that parallel the river. Floating is recommended as the best way to work this entire section of river. Take-out is either at Ashton (Wendell) Bridge on Highway 20 or at the boat ramp in the backwaters of Ashton Reservoir.

Pine Haven to Warm River

Types of Fish
Mostly rainbow trout with increasing numbers of brown trout below Mesa Falls.

Known Hatches
Salmonflies in June.

Flies to Use
Dry Patterns: Stonefly and standard dry flies.
Nymphs: Woolly Bugger and sculpin-type streamers.

When to Fish
Almost anytime, but the best fly fishing is during the salmonfly hatch in June.

Seasons & Limits
Seasons and limits can change, so consult the Idaho Fish & Game regulations, but generally from Ashton to Riverside Campground is open all year with a two-fish over 16" limit.

Rating
Because of the effort involved, a 5.

Warm River to Ashton

Types of Fish
Mostly rainbows with increasing numbers of browns.

Flies to Use
Dry Patterns: Humpy, Elk Hair Caddis, Stimulator, Henryville Caddis, Parachute Adams, Light Cahill, & Royal Wulff #12–16.
Nymphs & Terrestrials: Many wet or soft hackle patterns, Black Rubber Legs #6–8; Dave's Hopper #8–10.

When to Fish
All season, but this area can be especially good in August and early September when other areas go flat.

Seasons & Limits
Riverside Campground to Wendell bridge at Ashton: General season, two fish over 16" limit. Seasons and limits can change, so consult the Idaho Fish & Game regulations.

Rating
In early June, a 7. At most other times, a 5.

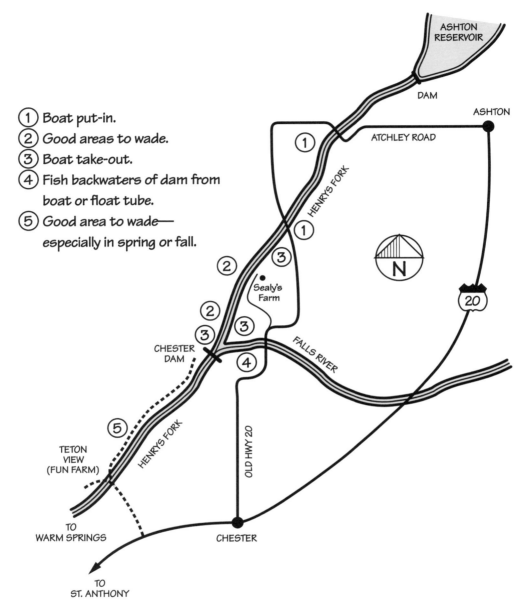

1. Boat put-in.
2. Good areas to wade.
3. Boat take-out.
4. Fish backwaters of dam from boat or float tube.
5. Good area to wade—especially in spring or fall.

ASHTON RESERVOIR

DAM

ASHTON

ATCHLEY ROAD

HENRYS FORK

N

20

Sealy's Farm

FALLS RIVER

CHESTER DAM

HENRYS FORK

OLD HWY 20

TETON VIEW (FUN FARM)

TO WARM SPRINGS

CHESTER

TO ST. ANTHONY

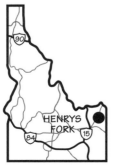

90

HENRYS FORK

84   15

HENRYS FORK

ASHTON DAM TO CHESTER ("SEALY'S")

NOT TO SCALE

Henrys Fork
Ashton Dam to Chester ("Sealy's")

This area is commonly referred to as "Sealy's" because of nearby Sealy's farm. Because it's open year-round and has catch limits, fly fishing is better than ever.

Getting to and finding the various fly fishing areas is easy. From Ashton, head west to Ora Bridge, just below Ashton Dam. Sealy's farm, above Chester Dam, is private property but has a public access area. Go to the small town of Chester, just off Highway 20. Take Chester Road across Falls River. Just after the road bends right, look for a dirt road on the left with fences and corrals. Look for a farmhouse in the distance on the right and tall stands of cottonwood trees bordering the river.

Because of limited access, floating is the best way to fish this section. If you are unfamiliar with this section of river or boating in general, consult a qualified guide or outfitter. The backwater of Chester Dam must be fished from a boat or float tube.

For the Chester Dam put-in or take-out, take Teton View Road just north of St. Anthony off Highway 20. Cross the river, turn right, and take the dirt road to the dam. To reach the Ashton Bridge put-in, at the traffic light in Ashton, turn west to Ashton Dam, cross the river, and put in below the bridge.

Types of Fish
Mostly rainbows with increasing numbers of brown trout.

Hatches & Flies to Use
March–April
Hatches can be very heavy. Be prepared to fish them all.
Dry Patterns: Midges, Early Blue-Winged Olive #18–20; Dirty Olive Caddis #14–16.

May–June
Spring runoff can stop most hatches but also heralds the salmonfly.
Dry Patterns: Improved Sofa Pillow #4–6; Adams, Adams Parachute #20; Black Midge Pupa, Brassie, Blue-Winged Olive, Light Olive Parachute, Gray/Olive No-Hackle #18–20; Lawson's Henry's Fork Salmon Fly #4–6.
Nymphs: Pheasant Tail, Mason Baetis Nymph #18; Olive Caddis #14–16; Salmon Fly #2–6.

June–July
The real fishing begins. Keep flies reasonably sparse.
Dry Patterns: Green/Gray Drake #10; Green Drake Paradun, Pale Morning Dun, Parachute PMD, Gray/Yellow No-Hackle, PMD Thorax #14–20. Also various Caddis #14–18; Red Quill Hen Spinner #10–12 (dry) for the backwaters of Chester Dam.

August
Can be slow.
September 15–October
The *Baetis* hatch is spectacular.
Dry Patterns: Blue-Winged Olive, Olive Parachute or Thorax, Slate Mahogany Dun. #18–20.

When to Fish
Early or late season is best. In mid to late summer, hatches diminish and weed growth and water levels are high, making fishing slow and technical. By late fall, the fishing becomes outstanding.

Seasons & Limits
Chester to Ashton Dam is generally open all year with a two-trout limit, none under 16". Seasons and limits can change, consult the Idaho Fish & Game regulations.

Rating
Overall, a 6.

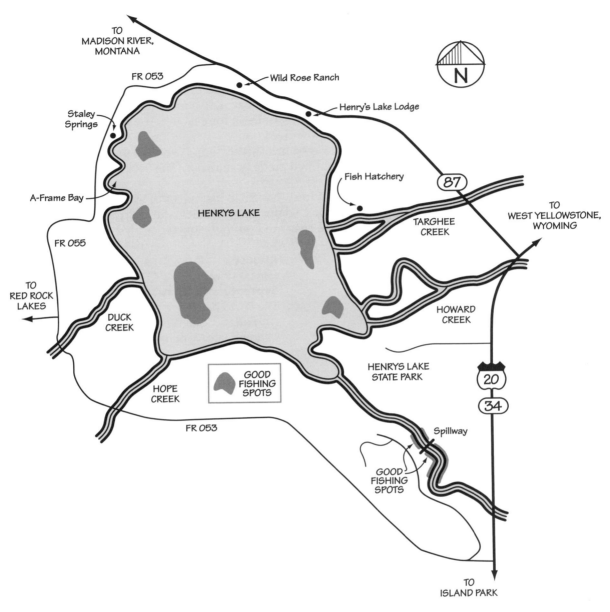

TO
MADISON RIVER,
MONTANA

FR 053

Wild Rose Ranch

N

Henry's Lake Lodge

Staley
Springs

Fish Hatchery

87

A-Frame Bay

HENRYS LAKE

TO
WEST YELLOWSTONE,
WYOMING

FR 055

TARGHEE
CREEK

TO
RED ROCK
LAKES

DUCK
CREEK

HOWARD
CREEK

GOOD
FISHING
SPOTS

HENRYS LAKE
STATE PARK

20

HOPE
CREEK

34

FR 053

Spillway

GOOD
FISHING
SPOTS

TO
ISLAND PARK

90

HENRYS
LAKE

15

84

HENRYS LAKE

NOT TO SCALE

46

Henrys Lake

Henrys Lake is probably the finest fly fishing lake in Idaho. If you know of a better one, you might want to keep it to yourself. The 4.5 by 3.5 mile lake is shallow, with an average depth of 18 feet. Much of the water comes from springs, and the lake's rich aquatic growth provides tremendous nourishment for fish.

The majority of fishing on "Hanks Pond" is done from a boat or float tube. Fly fishing from the bank or by wading is limited. And despite what appear to be rising fish, Henrys does not fish with dry flies. Leave your floating lines in your car.

The lake consistently produces large brook trout and is the source of the current Idaho record holder. Fall fishing for "Mr. Squaretail," dressed in his bright spawning colors, can be quite exciting. For that matter, fishing Henrys Lake is always a rewarding experience at any season.

The lake is in northeastern Idaho, about 18 miles from Yellowstone National Park on Route 20. From Ennis, Montana, take Highway 87 south about 60 miles.

Types of Fish
Cutthroats, Henry's original inhabitants, predominate, with brook trout and some hybrid cutbows.

Known Hatches
The main hatch is the green damsel in July.

Equipment to Use
Rod: 7 weight, 8½' to 9'.
Reels: Mechanical or palm drag.
Lines: Fast sinking, or slow sinking for shallow areas.
Leaders: 3x to 5x, 9'.
Wading: It is best to take a boat or float tube. When tubing use chest-high neoprene waders and fins. *Note:* Thunderstorms can develop suddenly in the area, and the shallow lake can become quite dangerous. I once got caught in a storm and barely got off the lake.

Flies to Use
Wet or Nymph Patterns: Brown Marabou or Ostrich Leech #4–6, Troth Olive Shrimp #8–12, Olive Damsel Nymph #8–10, Matuka Light and Dark Spruce, Woolly Bugger #8–10. A favorite pattern is one created by Seldon Jones. It's nameless, but sports a peacock body and fuzzy badger hair thorax capped with white raffia. Flies should be weighted and tied a bit bigger and longer than usual.

When to Fish
July through October is very good. Try the Glory Hole off Staley Springs, the area between Duck Creek and Hope Creek, and the water around A-Frame Bay and Howard Creek. Targhee Creek can be good in the fall.

Seasons & Limits
The general season is usually the Saturday of Memorial Day weekend to November 30, 5:00 a.m.–9:00 p.m. with a two-fish limit. The rules on hours may change in 2006. The areas around Staley Springs and Hatchery Creek are closed to fishing. For exact dates and times check the Idaho Fish & Game regulations.

Accommodations & Services
Lots of camping is available at Henrys Lake State Park, Staley Springs, and Wild Rose Ranch. Boat ramps and docks are available in A-Frame Bay, Howard Creek, and Staley Springs. Cabins can be rented at Henry's Lake Lodge. For other services head to the Island Park/Last Chance area.

Rating
Overall, a solid 8.

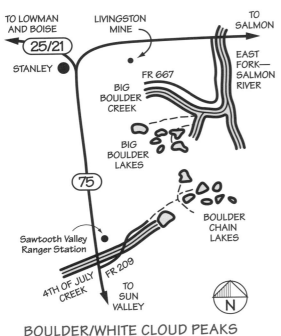

BOULDER/WHITE CLOUD PEAKS
AREA LAKES

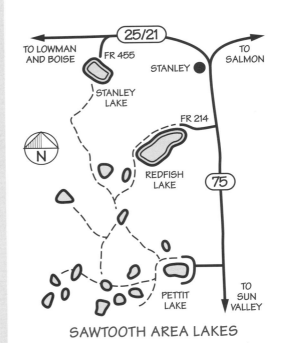

SAWTOOTH AREA LAKES

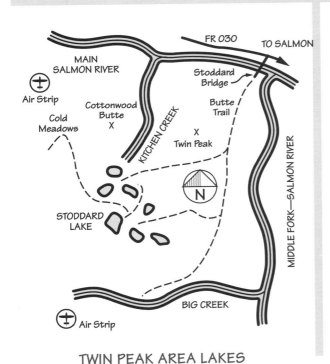

TWIN PEAK AREA LAKES

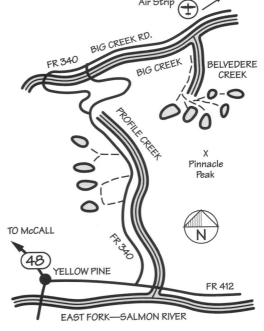

PINNACLE PEAK AREA LAKES

HIGH MOUNTAIN LAKES

NOT TO SCALE

High Mountain Lakes

If you like to hike or backpack and fly fish, Idaho offers some of the best and most picturesque high mountain lake fishing in the country. Generally the farther into the backcountry you go, the better your chances of finding large fish. With Idaho's beautiful mountain scenery, these fly fishing treks are worth the effort, large trout or not.

The majority of the high mountain lakes that are prime fly fishing destinations are located in the state's central wilderness area. Some are quite easy to get to whereas others require either horses or airplanes capable of landing on backcountry airstrips. See the accompanying maps for some of the best high mountain fly fishing lakes. NOTE: These maps are not to scale; show water locations only; carry a topographic map for locating routes.

Types of Fish

Most lakes are stocked with cutthroat, rainbow, brook, and golden trout. These populations may be high, but fish size can be small. Restocked every three years.

Known Hatches

At high altitude insect populations are decreased, but you'll find caddis (evenings), black midges (especially the pupa stage), freshwater shrimp, leeches, backswimmers, damsel flies, ants, and grasshoppers.

Equipment to Use

Rods: 5 to 7 weight, 8½' to 9'.
Reels: Palm drag.
Lines: Floating and sink tip for flexibility.
Leaders: 3x to 6x, 7½' to 9'.
Wading: Chest-high neoprene waders and a float tube are helpful if you want to pack them in.

Flies to Use

Dry Patterns: Parachute and regular Adams #14–20, Henryville Caddis #12–18, Dave's Hopper #10–12.
Nymphs: Black Midge Pupa #16–20, Olive Damsel #10–12, Brown Backswimmer #14–16, Shaggy Otter #12–16, Black, Brown, & Black/Olive Woolly Bugger #8–12.

When to Fish

Generally fly fish the high lakes in midsummer. By October, winter conditions can put an end to fishing.

Hiking

Check with the Forest Service for restrictions on fires and stoves. Always carry a topographic map of your hiking area. *Do not* use the maps in this book for hiking reference. They're for general use and are not to scale. Also, pack out what you take in.

Boulder/White Cloud Peaks Area

This area offers some of the finest back country fly fishing in Idaho, and the hike in is relatively easy. Because of nutrient-rich water, the various lakes are full of insects and hold some very big fish for such a high altitude.

The most common way in (and up) is via Fourth of July Creek, off Highway 75, south of Stanley. The other route is up the East Fork of the Salmon to Livingston Mine. This route, though a bit steeper, provides access to Big Boulder Creek and Lakes, and Boulder Chain Lakes. This area does get a lot of visitors, but the jaunt through this mountain range is beautiful and something you will never forget.
Rating: As high lakes go, a 7.5.

The Sawtooth Range

These beautiful granite mountains are often called "America's Alps." When you round the bend into lower Stanley, the Sawtooths literally explode in your face, presenting a sight that anyone with a sense of the spectacular will always enjoy. This area can get a lot of use in peak season. Common access points are Pettit, Redfish, and Stanley lakes. Pettit gets my nod.
Rating: A 4.

Continued on page 50

Continued from page 49

Twin Peak

This area, deep in the wilderness of central Idaho, goes by many names: Cottonwood Butte/Stoddard Lake Region, Big Creek, or Chamberlain Basin. To simplify things, and because of the two landmark pinnacles, Twin Peak is my designation.

Lakes in this area, including Stoddard, Kitchen, Cottonwood, and Basin, are remote and feature high-quality water and some of the largest backcountry trout in the state. Cutthroats and rainbows of 20 inches or more (unheard of in many other high-altitude lakes) can be quite common. Try fishing Big Creek for surprisingly large cutthroats.

Probably the best way to reach this area is by horse. From Stoddard Bridge, which crosses the Salmon River, it's a day's ride (or more). Hiking takes a couple of days at more than 5,500 feet in elevation. Save your time, take a horse, you'll love it. You can fly into Cold Meadow, though that still leaves you with a day's hike into the lakes. You can also fly into Big Creek and hike in from the south. An area fly shop can help you with these arrangements.

Rating: The fly fishing is a 10. The trip in, especially if you are hiking, makes it a 5.5.

Pinnacle Peak Area

I've been very close to these lakes, but because of weather, haven't fished them. Friends who have completed the trek and fly fished this area give it high marks: good trout 16 to 17 inches and lots in the 10- to 12-inch range.

To get to the trail, follow the Forest Roads 412 and 340 out of Yellow Pine and up Profile Creek to Big Creek. The trailhead is where the road crosses Belvedere Creek. On the map, the lakes appear close, but the 3,000-foot climb can take up to a day and a half. Word has it this can be cut in half by taking Profile Creek over Coin Mountain. In my estimation, this route is for the young and fit.

Rating: From reports, a 6.5.

Pioneer Area Lakes

Consider these lakes for a convenient day trip from the Sun Valley—Ketchum area. The mountains and lakes can be reached in a few hours. Some lakes hold trout 8 to 10 inches; others don't contain fish at all. But the trip is nice.

Take Trail Creek Road (FR408) north and east from Ketchum. Turn right on East Fork Road (FR135). Either look for trail heads off it or turn off on to Wildhorse Creek Road (FR136). Continuing along East Fork road also brings you to Copper Basin Loop Road (FR138)

Rating: A 3.5.

Kelly Creek

Kelly Creek is one of the great trout streams in northern Idaho's panhandle region. Special catch and release regulations have helped save the stream's indigenous cutthroat trout, though overall it does lack the big fish associated with many blue ribbon streams. A strong population of catchable fish in the 10-to 15-inch category, with the occasional larger fish, is reason enough to head for Kelly Creek.

Kelly Creek can be reached from the north from Superior, Montana. Most approach from the west via Lewiston or Orofino. Go through the little town of Pierce, Idaho, taking State Highway 11. After some 45 miles (on Forest Road 250, a good dirt road) look for signs that direct you to the Kelly Creek Ranger Station, where a road parallels the creek.

Types of Fish
Westslope cutthroat.

Equipment to Use
Rods: 4 to 6 weight, 8½' to 9'.
Reels: Mechanical or palm drag.
Lines: Floating line to match your rod weight. Use split shot to fish nymphs.
Leaders: 4x and 5x, 9' to 12'.
Wading: Neoprene waders with felt-soled wading shoes or hip boots.

Flies to Use
Dry Patterns: Yellow and Olive Stimulators, Royal Wulff, & Elk Hair Caddis #12–16; grasshopper patterns #8–10.
Nymphs: Prince or Hare's Ear, regular and beaded #10–16; Flashback, Small Woolly Buggers #12–16.

When to Fish
Depending on snowpack, runoff may delay the good fishing until mid-July. Fall is the best time to fly fish Kelly Creek.

Seasons & Limits
Catch & release, barbless hooks on artificial flies and lures. Check the Idaho Fish & Game regulations.

Accommodations & Services
There is a Forest Service campground with basic facilities at the stream, but no other services are in the area.

Rating
A solid 7.5.

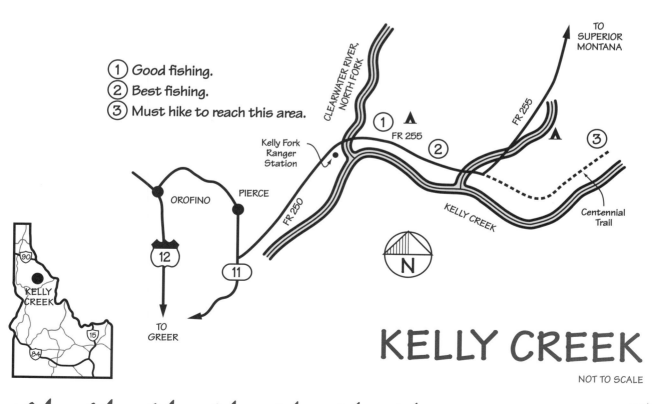

1. Good fishing.
2. Best fishing.
3. Must hike to reach this area.

KELLY CREEK

NOT TO SCALE

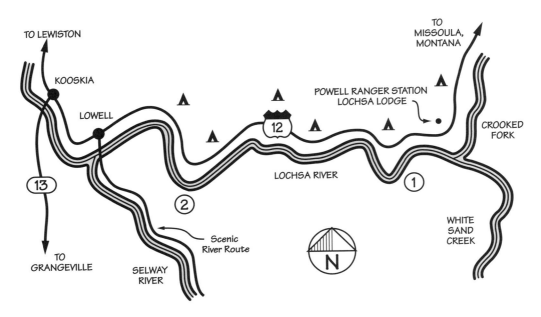

① Catch and release section from Gateway Bridge to Powell. Best fly fishing section.

② Two-fish limit in this area.

Note: Best fly fishing in summer and fall.
Many campgrounds and RV facilities all along river.

LOCHSA RIVER

NOT TO SCALE

Lochsa River

The Lochsa is very accessible when you're in the northern part of the state. The Lewis and Clark Highway (Highway 12) parallels this fairly large river most of the way, making access fairly routine. The towns of Lowell and Powell are at the ends of this portion of the Lochsa.

The 30-mile upper river from Powell to Wilderness Gateway Campground Bridge is catch and release and the best bet for fly fishing success. The 50-mile lower river from the Wilderness Gateway Bridge to Lowell has good quantities of insects but fewer fish than the upper section.

Limits and catch and release regulations were placed on the Lochsa in an effort to maintain the Westslope cutthroat trout. The results are lots of trout between 12 and 14 inches and many in the 18-inch category.

Types of Fish
Primarily cutthroat with some rainbow trout.

Known Hatches
Mayflies
September: Little cream dun (*Centroptilum*), slate mahogany dun (*Paraleptophlebia*).
Stoneflies
April–May: Golden stone.

Equipment to Use
Rods: 5 to 6 weight, 8½' to 9'.
Reels: Mechanical or palm drag.
Lines: Floating line to match rod weight.
Leaders: 4x to 6x, 9'.
Wading: Chest-high neoprene waders with felt-soled wading shoes. High water in the spring can make wading difficult.

Flies to Use
Dry Patterns: Royal Wulff, Stimulator, Elk Hair Caddis, Adams, Parachute Adams, & Light Cahill #12–18; Little Cream Dun #20; Slate Mahogany Dun #10–12; Golden Stone #8; Yellow Stimulator #6–8.
Nymphs: Prince, Hare's Ear, Brown Stone Fly #10–14.

When to Fish
The best fly fishing is in the late summer and fall. During the whitefish season before spring runoff, try the lower sections.

Season & Limits
General season, with a two-trout limit (at least 14") below the wilderness boundary. The upper river is catch and release. Artificial lures and barbless hooks only. Seasons and rules change so refer to the Idaho Fish & Game regulations.

Accommodations & Services
There are various campground and RV facilities throughout the region. Hotels, motels, service stations, grocery stores, and other services can be found in Lowell and Powell.

Rating
A solid 8 in the fall.

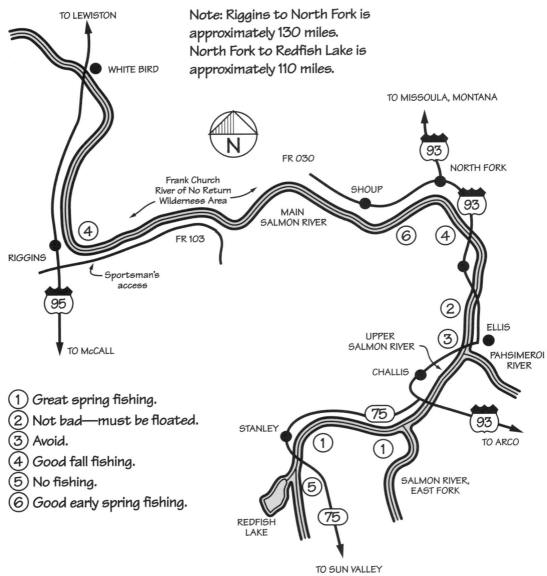

TO LEWISTON

WHITE BIRD

Note: Riggins to North Fork is approximately 130 miles. North Fork to Redfish Lake is approximately 110 miles.

TO MISSOULA, MONTANA

93

FR 030

NORTH FORK

93

Frank Church River of No Return Wilderness Area

SHOUP

MAIN SALMON RIVER

6 4

4

FR 103

RIGGINS

Sportsman's access

95

2

ELLIS

UPPER SALMON RIVER

PAHSIMEROI RIVER

TO McCALL

3

CHALLIS

1 Great spring fishing.
2 Not bad—must be floated.
3 Avoid.
4 Good fall fishing.
5 No fishing.
6 Good early spring fishing.

75

STANLEY

1

1

93

TO ARCO

SALMON RIVER, EAST FORK

5

REDFISH LAKE

75

TO SUN VALLEY

SALMON RIVER

MAIN & UPPER

NOT TO SCALE

SALMON RIVER, MAIN & UPPER

Salmon River, Main & Upper

From its origins in the Sawtooth range, the upper Salmon flows north through the mountains to the small village of North Fork, a distance of about 170 miles. The river then heads west on a 450-mile journey of whitewater and runs going through the rugged canyons and mountains of the 2.25 million acre Frank Church River of No Return Wilderness Area. This middle section is best fished from a boat. The Salmon eventually meets the Snake River at Hell's Canyon on the Idaho-Oregon border. For us fly fishers, the upper and main sections are the most interesting.

The upper section is paralleled by Highway 75, which affords good river access. Part of the middle section, from North Fork to Corn Creek, has varying degrees of road and river access. From Corn Creek downriver it's pretty much boat only.

To get to the upper section of the Salmon, take Highway 75 from Sun Valley/Ketchum and Stanley. Or from eastern Idaho, take any highway to Arco and then get on Highway 93 north to Challis.

Mountain scenery and wilderness aside, the steelhead runs now get most of the attention when considering this river. Hatchery and wild steelhead return from the sea in September, some running up to 20 pounds. If you are new to this river or to steelheading, hiring a competent local guide would be a worthwhile investment.

A selection of trouts including Dolly Vardens (bull trout) up to 20 inches offer some fly fishing challenges, though they receive less notoriety than their sea-running cousins. There are more than enough fish in this river to please the fly angler.

Types of Fish

Steelhead during their spawning runs, whitefish, rainbows, some bull trout, cutthroats, and steelhead smolt can make fly fishing here rewarding for everyone.

Equipment to Use

Trout:
Rods: 4 to 7 weight, 8½' to 9½'.
Reels: Palm drag is fine.
Lines: Floating and sinktip lines to match rod.
Leaders: 4x or 5x, 9'.

Steelhead:
Rods: 6 to 9 weight, 9' to 9½'.
Reels: Mechanical drag.
Lines: Both floating and sink tiplines to match rod weight.
Leaders: 0x or 1x, 7' to 9'.
Wading: Chest-high neoprenes with felt-soled wading shoes, stream cleats, and a wading staff. Consider floating below Challis.

Flies to Use

Trout
General patterns such as Royal Wulff, Humpy, Elk Hair Caddis, & Caddis Pupa in sizes #12–14; Dave's Hopper #8–10.

Steelhead
Fall: Green Butted Skunk, Skykomish Sunrise, Silver Hilton, Thor's & Egg Sucking Black Leech, Purple Peril, Marabou Wing, & Hair Wing #4–8.

Spring: Add to fall patterns a small egg pattern in cream, burnt orange, or light pink #8–10.

When to Fish

About April 1 fly fishing starts getting good between the East Fork of the Salmon and Redfish Lake. In the fall, most of the fish are found from the Riggins/White Bird area upstream to the city of Salmon. Jet boats and the wide, deep river make the White Bird area and the section between the cities of North Fork and Salmon the best places to fly fish. *Note:* A major hatchery and collection point for returning fish is located at the confluence of the Pahsimeroi and Salmon Rivers at Ellis. This area can be a real fly fishing circus.

Seasons & Limits

The season and limits are different for trout and steelhead, so consult the Idaho Fish & Game regulations. The steelhead season is usually September 15 to November 30 and March 20 to April 30. In spring be careful to avoid walking through spawning areas and beds. Six hatchery trout may be kept.

Accommodation and Services

Supplies and very adequate accommodations are available in Salmon, Challis, Stanley, and Riggins. Once the snow melts, campgrounds are available up and down the river.

Rating

For spring steelhead a solid 8. For trout a 2.5.

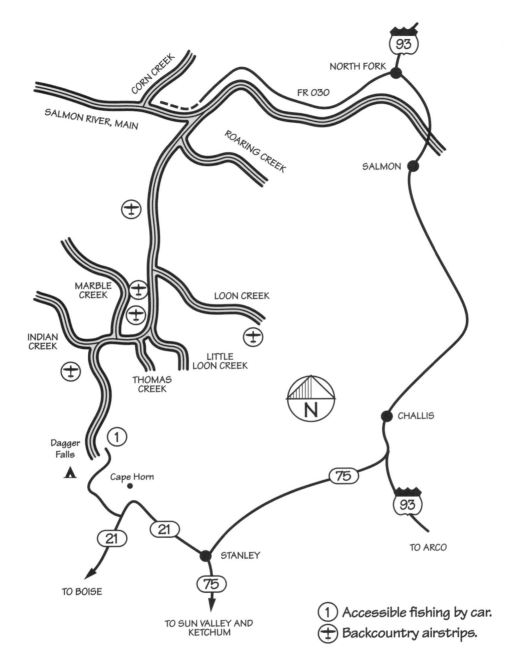

CORN CREEK

93

NORTH FORK

FR 030

SALMON RIVER, MAIN

ROARING CREEK

SALMON

MARBLE CREEK

LOON CREEK

INDIAN CREEK

LITTLE LOON CREEK

THOMAS CREEK

N

CHALLIS

Dagger Falls

1

Cape Horn

75

93

21

21

TO ARCO

STANLEY

TO BOISE

75

TO SUN VALLEY AND KETCHUM

1 Accessible fishing by car.

Backcountry airstrips.

SALMON RIVER

MIDDLE FORK

NOT TO SCALE

90

SALMON RIVER, MIDDLE FORK

15

84

Salmon River, Middle Fork

Through this pristine, scenic wilderness flow crystal clear waters that now contain an abundance of Westslope cutthroat trout. Overfishing nearly depleted the cutthroats, but catch and release regulations placed in effect in 1970 have restored the fish to near overpopulation. Now the most novice fly fisher will catch fish from this beautiful river.

A portion of the river can be reached via Highway 21 from Stanley by taking the gravel road to Dagger Falls. The remaining 100 miles can only be accessed by boat, or by small plane using various mountain airstrips. If you plan to fly in, contact an experienced backcountry pilot.

Difficulty of access and lack of crowds are two reasons the Middle Fork is one of the most popular three- to six-day whitewater float trips in Idaho. You'll need a Forest Service permit (Salmon, ID) to do this, or take a trip with an outfitter. Hiring an outfitter is good idea. With class 2 to 4 rapids the Middle Fork is not for the inexperienced.

Types of Fish

Primarily cutthroats, some steelhead and steelhead smolts, and a few rainbows.

Equipment to Use

Rods: 5 to 6 weight, 8' to 9½'.
Reels: Palm or mechanical drag.
Line: Floating line to match rod weight.
Leaders: 4x to 5x, 9'.
Wading: Chest-high neoprene waders with felt-soled wading shoes.

Flies to Use

When people ask what flies to use here, I jokingly say "Yes." More precisely, take the following: Royal Wulff #14, Yellow Humpy #14, Elk Hair Caddis #10–14, Golden Stone #10, Dave's Hopper #8.

When to Fish

Early-season runoff can affect conditions, but generally, starting July 4 the river fishes well. From August 1 to season's end is prime.

Seasons & Limits

Most sections open all year, except the mouth of the Middle Fork to Roaring Creek which is open Memorial Day weekend to September 30. The Middle Fork is barbless, catch and release only. Different regulations for steelhead. Consult the Idaho Fish & Game regulations.

Accommodations & Services

Riverside camping only. This is remote fly fishing, bring whatever you need and pack it out.

Rating

An 8.5, only because it lacks large fish.

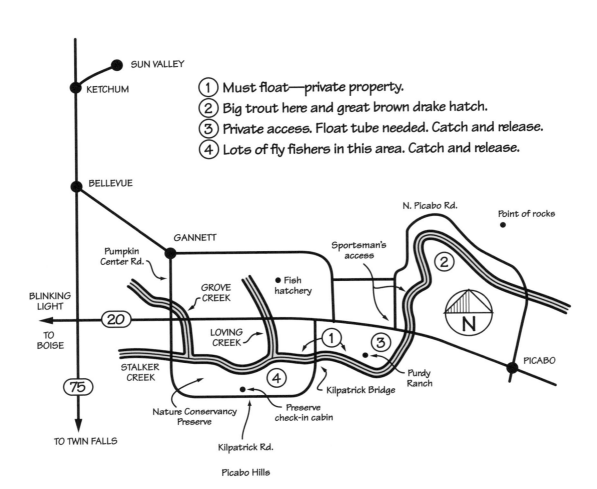

① Must float—private property.
② Big trout here and great brown drake hatch.
③ Private access. Float tube needed. Catch and release.
④ Lots of fly fishers in this area. Catch and release.

SUN VALLEY

KETCHUM

BELLEVUE

N. Picabo Rd.

Point of rocks

GANNETT

Sportsman's access

Pumpkin Center Rd.

GROVE CREEK

Fish hatchery

BLINKING LIGHT

20

TO BOISE

LOVING CREEK

75

STALKER CREEK

Purdy Ranch

PICABO

Kilpatrick Bridge

Nature Conservancy Preserve

Preserve check-in cabin

Kilpatrick Rd.

Picabo Hills

TO TWIN FALLS

SILVER CREEK

NOT TO SCALE

Note: Silver Creek is 35 miles from Sun Valley.

Silver Creek

Internationally famous, "The Creek," as locals refer to it, is perhaps the finest piece of dry fly water you can find. It's also one of the largest, purest spring-fed streams in this country. Silver Creek's abundant food supply supports numerous large trout, to which the fly presentation must be near perfect. Moreover, fly imitations must be precise in size, color, and profile. Sound challenging? It is.

In the upper section of Silver Creek within the Nature Conservancy Preserve, trout and fly fishers are abundant. The Purdy Ranch section, downstream from the preserve, is private. Here the trout population is very strong, but a float tube is required to reach them. The Point of Rocks area has very big trout, though fewer in numbers than in the other sections. This is the brown drake hatch area. Bear in mind that I have tried to condense the basic information needed to fly fish all sections of this complicated water on a single page.

From Sun Valley/Ketchum take Highway 75, 35 miles south to Gannet, where signs direct you to the Nature Conservancy Preserve. Other sections of river are reached off of Highway 20. To reach them, turn east at the flashing signal light at the intersection of Highways 75 and 20.

Types of Fish
Rainbow, brown, and some brook trout.

Known Hatches
See Hatch Chart on page 14.

Equipment to Use
Rods: 3 to 5 weight, 8½' to 9'.
Reels: Mechanical or palm drag.
Lines: Floating.
Leaders: 5x to 7x with 8x for small mayflies.
Wading: Chest-high neoprene waders and felt-soled wading boots.

Flies to Use (See Hatch Chart page 14)
June 1 to 10: Imitate the brown drake hatch in the Point of Rocks area with Duns and Spinners at dusk. *Dry Patterns:* Brown Drake, Paradrake, & Partridge Spinner #10; Pale Morning Dun #16–18. *Nymphs:* Brown Drake #10.
June–August 15: Pale morning duns peak the first week of August. Duns emerge July–Aug. at dusk. To June 1–10 flies add Gray/Yellow No-Hackle, Parachute Pale Morning Dun, & Yellow Hen Spinner #6–18.
June–September: Late-morning hatch of light olive quill spinner. Mayfly hatch continuous. Peak hatch of speckled dun and spinner 8/25–9/20. To June–Aug. 15 flies add *Dry:* Little Olive Quill Spinner, Mason Loopwing Spinner, Red Quill Hen Spinner, Light Olive Parachute & Gray/Yellow No-Hackle #22; Gray Partridge Parachute, & Slate/Gray No-Hackle #22; Partridge Hen Spinner #18–20. *Nymphs:* Red Quill Emerger tied sparsely, Callibaetis #14–18.
July 20–August: Big morning trico spinner falls. To June–Sept., add Trico or White-Winged Black #22, White/Black CDC Spinner #22, White/Black Hen Spinner, Mason Loopwing Trico, & White/Black No-Hackle #22.
August 15–September 10: Late-morning and early afternoon small pale morning dun hatch. To July 20–Aug. flies add Small PMD, PMD Parachute, & Gray/Yellow No-Hackle #20.
August 25–September 1: Sporadic afternoon *Baetis* hatch. To Aug. 15–Sept. 10 flies above, add Little Bright Olive Dun, Little Olive Parachute #22, Speckled Dun, & Spinner #16–20.
September 20–October: Afternoon blue-winged olive hatch. *Dry Patterns:* Blue-Winged Olive #20, Little Olive Parachute and Gray/Olive No-Hackle #20. *Nymphs:* Mason Baetis Nymph #18, Pheasant Tail #18.
October: Inconsistent but good slate mahogany dun or *Paraleptophlebia* hatch. To Sept. 20–Oct. flies add Slate Mahogany Dun Paralep, No-Hackle, & Brown Parachute, #16.

When to Fish
You can fish summer through winter, but the best fishing is midsummer into late fall. Hatches can be inconsistent in June.

Seasons & Limits
Consult the Idaho Fish & Game regulations. Nature Conservancy and Purdy Ranch areas are catch and release, barbless hooks, no bait, no boats. Below Highway 20 is a two-fish limit, none between 12" and 16".

Accommodations & Services
Some camping is available at the Fish & Game hatchery and the Point of Rocks sportsman's access area. Find plenty of lodging and services 25–35 miles north on Highway 75 in the towns of Hailey, Ketchum, and Sun Valley or 60 miles south on Highway 75 in Twin Falls.

Rating
For classic dry fly fishing in a challenging situation, Silver Creek is a solid 10.

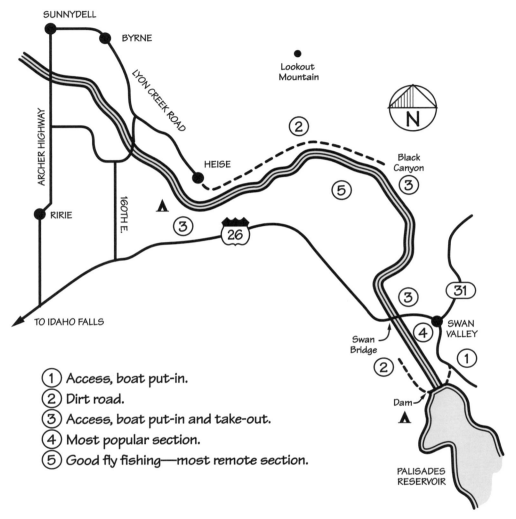

SUNNYDELL
BYRNE
LYON CREEK ROAD
Lookout Mountain
ARCHER HIGHWAY
HEISE
160TH E.
RIRIE
Black Canyon
②
⑤
③
26
③
TO IDAHO FALLS
③
31
③
④ SWAN VALLEY
Swan Bridge
①
②
Dam
PALISADES RESERVOIR

① Access, boat put-in.
② Dirt road.
③ Access, boat put-in and take-out.
④ Most popular section.
⑤ Good fly fishing—most remote section.

SNAKE RIVER, SOUTH FORK

SNAKE RIVER
SOUTH FORK
NOT TO SCALE

Snake River, South Fork

The South Fork of the Snake River, all 60 miles of it, is one of the great river systems in the state of Idaho. Starting in Wyoming, the South Fork's fertile and rowdy waters produce huge fish. Fly fishers can cast to some of the largest cutthroat and brown trout in Idaho. The state record brown (some 35 pounds) was taken from these waters.

Most of the great fly fishing is in two sections: From Palisades Dam 10 miles downstream to Swan Valley Bridge and from Swan Valley Bridge to Black Canyon or Table Rock. The former section has easier access, is a shorter float, and hence, is the more popular. The lower section is just as good but more remote. This river is very popular, and you had better be prepared to share the water with other people and boats during the peak season.

The South Fork is big water, and although it can be waded in most spots, the most practical way to fish the river is by boat. There is a salmonfly hatch around mid-July that moves four or five miles upstream each day, which can send trout into a feeding frenzy. It can provide some fantastic fly fishing. Salmonfly hatch or not, a day fly fishing on the South Fork will be a day long remembered.

The easiest way to reach the South Fork of the Snake is to take Highway 26 from Idaho Falls toward Jackson Hole, Wyoming. Cross the South Fork or the Swan Valley Bridge, then drive upstream along the river to Palisades Dam. Take-outs in the lower section can be accessed by passing through the small community of Sunnydell and traveling upstream to Table Rock and Black Canyon.

Types of Fish
Cutthroats, German browns, some rainbows, a few mackinaws that sneak in from the reservoir, and mountain whitefish.

Known Hatches
Brief mid-July salmonfly hatch.

Equipment to Use
Rods: 6 to 8 weight, 9'.
Reels: Mechanical or palm drag.
Lines: Floating or sink tip to match rod weight.
Leaders: 1x to 5x, 7'–9'.
Wading: Chest-high neoprene waders with felt-soled wading shoes. The South Fork of the Snake has some treacherous sections, so be very careful when wading.

Flies to Use
Dry Patterns: Parachute Adams & Light Cahill #8–18; Elk Hair & Henryville Caddis #12–16; Soft Hackle flies for the emerging pupa and Grasshoppers #12–16.
Wet Patterns: Super Renegade, Black, Black & Olive, & Brown Variegated Woolly Buggers #2–6; Jansen's Little Rainbow Trout #8.
July Salmonfly Hatch: Henry's Fork Stone & Bird's Stonefly #4–8; Black Rubber Leg Nymph #4–6.

When to Fish
The mid-July Salmonfly hatch is great but of limited duration. High water can be a problem in the summer. With more consistent water levels, September and October have great fish and may offer the best fall fly fishing in the state.

Seasons & Limits
Open year-round. No limit on rainbows and hybrids; two brown trout 16" or over; cutthroat are catch and release. Check the Idaho Department of Fish & Game regulations for updates.

Accommodations & Services
Camping, car parks, boat launches, and other facilities are scattered along most of the river. Motels and lodges are available in Idaho Falls and Swan Valley. Luxury accommodations are available at Palisade Resort Lodge.

Rating
In the late summer and especially the fall, this river rates a solid 10. Midsummer, with the exception of the salmonfly hatch, high and inconsistent water levels can drop it to a 6.5.

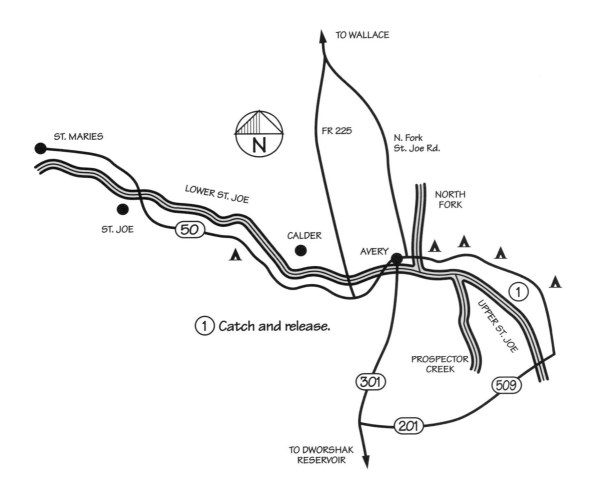

ST. JOE RIVER

NOT TO SCALE

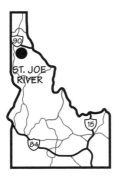

St. Joe River

The section of the St. Joe from the town of Avery to the headwaters is designated a Wild and Scenic River. The eastern stretch of river is a Wild Trout Trophy Fishery. The lower sections feature fine bass fishing. Residents of northern Idaho consider the St. Joe one of the best rivers to fish in the entire state.

The lower river, between St. Maries and Prospector Creek is big water, making wading fairly difficult. The smaller upper section can be waded except for the many deep pools. In addition, you must often maneuver around or cast from house-sized boulders. This is not a fly fishing river for youngsters or for people with difficulty getting around. This aside, the river and surrounding area are beautiful, and if you are in the northern part of Idaho in midsummer or fall, be sure to visit the St. Joe.

From southern Idaho, go to St. Maries (south of Lake Coeur d'Alene) and take Highway 5 to St. Maries and then Highway 50 up the river. From the north take Interstate 90 to Wallace, Idaho. In town turn south on the road leading to Avery. From Avery, you can drive up and down river.

Types of Fish
Primarily cutthroat, with some Dolly Vardens and bass in the lower sections.

Equipment to Use
Rods: 5 to 6 weight, 8½' to 9'.
Reels: Palm or mechanical drag.
Lines: Floating and sinktip lines to match rod weight.
Leaders: 3x to 5x, 7½' to 9'.
Wading: Chest-high neoprene waders with felt-soled wading shoes.

Flies to Use
Dry Patterns: Royal Wulff, Humpy, Stimulator, Elk Hair Caddis #12–16.
Nymphs: Prince Nymph and Hares Ear #10–14; Black, Brown and Black/Olive Flashabou Woolly Bugger #8–12.

When to Fish
Because of runoff, good fishing does not begin until mid-July. As water levels drop fishing improves.

Seasons & Limits
Generally from the town of St. Maries upstream to Avery there is a two-cutthroat limit (must be over 16"). Above Avery the river is catch and release, with barbless hooks and artificial flies and lures. The season usually runs from Memorial Day weekend to November 30. Seasons and limits can change, so consult the Idaho Fish & Game regulations.

Accommodations & Services
Campgrounds are located up and down the river, but tend to get smaller as you move upstream. Services, food, gas, etc., are available at Avery and St. Maries.

Rating
A 6.5.

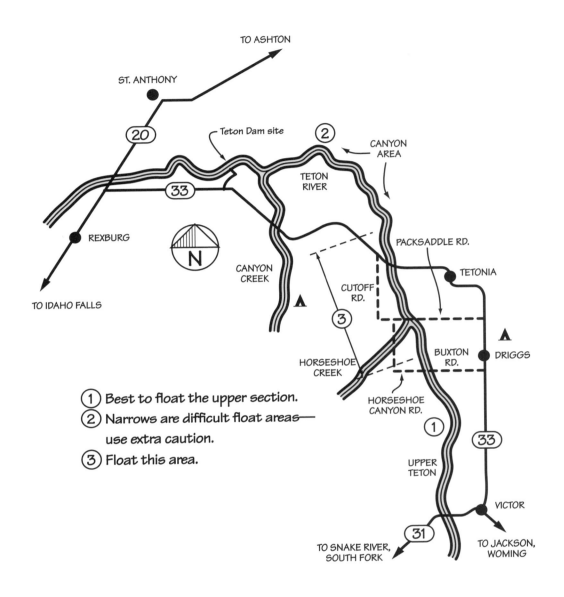

TO ASHTON

ST. ANTHONY

20

Teton Dam site

2

CANYON AREA

TETON RIVER

33

REXBURG

N

TO IDAHO FALLS

CANYON CREEK

PACKSADDLE RD.

TETONIA

CUTOFF RD.

3

BUXTON RD.

DRIGGS

HORSESHOE CREEK

HORSESHOE CANYON RD.

1

33

① Best to float the upper section.
② Narrows are difficult float areas—
   use extra caution.
③ Float this area.

UPPER TETON

VICTOR

31

TO SNAKE RIVER, SOUTH FORK

TO JACKSON, WOMING

90

15

TETON RIVER

84

TETON RIVER

NOT TO SCALE

Teton River

If you are in eastern Idaho or northwestern Wyoming and are looking for a smooth meadow-type stream with good insect activity and rising trout, try the Teton. If you're looking for an exciting, fast-flowing canyon-type river, the Teton is also a good bet. A bit of historical background is important, however, in evaluating this river.

The Teton was once one of eastern Idaho's greatest fly fishing streams. A series of problems, including poor farming and ranching practices, siltation, and the failure of the Teton Dam in 1976 changed the river drastically. Since the dam failure and resulting flood, reclamation funds have helped restore the upper meadow section and the canyon above the original damsite.

This canyon section, or "The Narrows," still has some very good fishing above the backwaters of the dam (Bitch Creek). It's a treacherous float, however. As Rene Harrop, the famous fly tier from St. Anthony says, "It still claims more McKenzie River drift boats per mile than any other river I know." Below the dam can be just as tricky. By all accounts the upper Teton should continue to improve and, I hope surpass its former glory.

The easiest way to reach Teton River is to take Highway 33 east from Rexburg (or west from Jackson Wyoming) to Driggs, Idaho. Look for the Sportsman's Access signs on Highway 33.

Types of Fish
Primarily cutthroat and rainbow trout.

Equipment to Use
Rods: 3 to 6 weight, with 6 weight preferred on the lower river, 8' to 9½'.
Reels: Mechanical or palm drag.
Lines: Match floating line to rod weight.
Leaders: 5x to 7x, 9' to 12'.
Wading: Chest-high neoprene waders and felt-soled wading boots. Wading is possible, but for the best fly fishing (given high silt accumulations), most of the upper Teton should be floated.

Flies to Use
Canyon Section
Dry Patterns: Henry's Fork Golden Stone (June), Yellow and Olive Stimulator #8–10; Elk Hair Caddis #12–16; Dave's Regular and Parachute Hopper, and other standard dries.
Nymphs: Golden stone.

Meadow Section
Dry Patterns: Pale Morning Dun #16–20; Parachute Pale Morning Dun, Thorax Pale Morning Dun, Gray/Yellow No-Hackle, Harrop Hair-Wing Dun, Little Olive Parachute in appropriate sizes, & Blue Winged Olive #18–22; Black or Brown Ant #8–14, Black Crowe Beetle #14–18, Yellow and Green Dave's Hopper Henry's Fork Hopper #8–12.
Nymphs: Mason Baetis & Pheasant Tail #18, Various Caddis #16–20; Tan, Black, Olive Partridge Caddis #14–20.

When to Fish
Mid-July to the end of August is the best fly fishing period.

Seasons & Limits
The general season is July 1 through November 30. Regulations can change, so consult the Idaho Fish & Game regulations.

Accommodations and Services
Lodging, camping, food, gas, and groceries are available in Driggs.

Rating
Because of stream degradation, a 4.5 to 5. If reclamation succeeds, a 7.5.

Additional Fishing Areas

More Lakes & Reservoirs

Some of the lakes and reservoirs in Idaho fall into this "honorable mention" section because of drought, declining water quality, lack of large trout, access problems, or other issues. Nonetheless, these waters are or have been good and are worth a try.

Island Park Reservoir

I have always loved fishing the fertile waters of Island Park Reservoir. I've spent many a memorable August afternoon at the west end, fishing in and off the "finger" areas. Trout of up to 20 inches were plentiful and fairly easy to catch. But the reservoir has suffered problems, including drawdowns. I'm not sure what size of fish are swimming around the reservoir now.

Access to the reservoir is quite easy. Most come in from McCrea's bridge on Shotgun Valley Road. A boat and motor are needed to access the reservoir downstream from this point. I think the best fishing is at the west end, reached from Green Canyon Road (FR167 continuing past Harriman State Park Headquarters) just south of Osborne bridge. If it is "on" Island Park Reservoir is worth a try. At the very least inquire at the fly shops in Last Chance.

Wet and Nymph Patterns: Brown, Marabou, or Ostrich Leech #4–6; Troth Olive Shrimp #8–12; Olive Damsel Nymph #8–10; Matuka Light and Dark Spruce & Woolly Bugger #8–10. Flies should be weighted more and tied longer than usual. Add Caddis pupa imitations when fishing the finger areas.

Lake Cascade

Cascade, near McCall, 80 miles north of Boise, is probably Idaho's most fished impoundment. Some very large trout are taken here, especially in the spring after ice-out. Most of the fish caught in the summer are hatchery raised. Water quality problems may affect the fishery, though time will tell. The reservoir should not be counted out, however, as the beauty of the area alone provides great enjoyment for anglers.

Lake Lowell

Located three miles southeast of Nampa, Idaho, Lake Lowell receives raves for its bass and bluegill fishing. Water conditions can change from year to year, however, making fly fishing inconsistent. From early to midsummer, grass and weed growth can make fly fishing relatively unrewarding. With bass in the four- to six-pound range and two-pound crappie, it's hard to argue against fly fishing here. If you're in the area, especially in the late spring when conditions elsewhere are marginal, consider Lake Lowell.

Flies to Use: Brown Ostrich or Marabou Nymph #4–6; small Leech, small Lead Head Jig, small Girdle Bug in black, brown, bright olive, chartreuse, and yellow #8–10; Foam Spider, Cricket, small Popping Bugs in black, green, yellow, and white #10–12 (#8–10 for crappie). For bass, Flashabou Woolly Bugger, beaded eyes or regular, in a variety of colors. Also try streamer patterns imitating chubs and a yellow or black perch imitation tied Matuka style.

Mackay Reservoir

This is a very interesting piece of water. It's fed by the Big Lost River and an assortment of area spring creeks that send high-quality water into the impoundment. The resident trout can be 20-plus inches. With better water and fishing regulation, Mackay could probably rival Henrys Lake as the top reservoir in the state.

Droughts have caused severe drawdowns, which tend to concentrate the fish. With few fishing restrictions the trout populations get tested severely, making it hard to predict what kind of fishing to expect.

Access is off Highway 93 which parallels its length. The reservoir can be fished from the bank, especially on the west side, but a boat or float tube is the preferred method. July can be very good in the northern end near the shallow backwaters. In and around the mouths of creeks can be good as well.

Flies to Use: Gray Drake Nymph, Brown Leech, Black, Brown, and Tan Woolly Bugger.

Magic Reservoir

Located 30 miles south of Sun Valley and Ketchum, Magic has fertile water that can produce some very high quality rainbow and brown trout. You probably won't be catching a fish a minute here, but you will get into some real tackle-busters.

Drought conditions in the late 1980s and in 1990 have severely affected the reservoir's water supply and adversely affected the fishery. These days, guessing what trout you'll find and what the fishing will be like is a bit of a dice roll. But because this water can be quite rich, I would never cross it off the list, especially in the fall.

Flies to Use: Black, Brown, and Variegated Woolly Bugger, Black and Yellow Perch Wolly Bugger, Leech patterns, and Stayner Ducktail Nymph.

Salmon Falls Creek Reservoir

There is a variety of fish in this high desert lake: rainbows, browns, smallmouth bass, and crappie to name a few. But the walleye get all the attention.

I admit I do not have a lot of experience on

this water, though the days I have fished here were fruitful. I do have enough experience to conclude that this is not a particularly great place for anglers.

The reservoir is overwhelmingly long and somewhat narrow, and access to the immense shoreline is difficult. A boat is the best way to get around. A float tube limits your mobility unless you know exactly where the fish are—hopefully the lake's east side with road access. Wind can also be a problem.

Nonetheless, if you're looking for the best walleye fishing in Idaho, drive about 35 miles southwest of Twin Falls on Highway 93.

More Rivers, Streams, & Creeks

Idaho has many more rivers, streams, and creeks that can provide gratifying fly fishing. These "other" waters—for reasons including drought, declining water quality, lack of large trout, access problems and other issues—are not afforded detailed attention in this guide. They deserve mention, however, and one just might be the kind of place you've been looking for.

Falls River

Located in eastern Idaho between the towns of Ashton and St. Anthony, Falls River meets Henrys Fork just above Chester Dam. Although not well known, it, and especially its upper end, is one of the more productive rivers in this part of the state. The Falls has it all: quality trout, great hatches, and a wonderful salmonfly hatch in mid-June. Floating is the best way to access and fly fish the entire river. Guided float trips are not permitted.

Wading can be difficult. In fact, wading Falls River makes the Madison, the Box Canyon on Henrys Fork, and the South Fork of the Boise seem easy. The streambed is very slick, and felt-soled wading shoes and or stream cleats are necessary. Access to the lower river is not particularly easy either. But if you are a capable wader and can overcome some inconvenience, the upper reaches of Falls River can make a really good fly fishing outing. It's wise to check at area fly shops about access points before venturing forth.

Little Wood River

Located south of Silver Creek, its main source of water, the Little Wood River has beautiful pools, runs, and riffles leading one to believe this is a trout haven. Because it flows through hot desert, this fine river is best fished in the fall and late spring.

The Little Wood received plantings of brown trout in the early 1970s (the source of the browns

in Silver Creek today) that accompany the stream's rainbow trout population. In the fall, *Baetis* (blue-winged olives) appear in the afternoon, transforming a no-fish day into one that can yield surprisingly large trout. *Flies to Use:* Hopper, Woolly Bugger, and in the fall, Parachute Adams #16–18.

Selway River

Located high in the Selway/Bitterroot Wilderness Area, the Selway River can have a staggering trout population, with 18-inch cutthroat commonplace. The river, which enters the Lochsa River at Lowell, is also one of the most pristine fly fishing environments in Idaho.

The lower section is accessible from the confluence upstream to Selway Falls and all types of fishing methods with general fish limits are permitted. As a result, the lower section tends to be less productive. The best way to access and fly fish the more productive upper river is by floating. But floating is limited by a permit system (for the public and outfitters), and such a trip must be planned far in advance.

The river and put-in site can be reached from the long and winding Magruder Corridor Road out of Darby, Montana. The easiest and quickest way in is to fly into Moose Creek a 6,000' Forest Service airstrip used for firefighting. Unfortunately, you are still limited to only a few parts of the river. Also, watch for rattlesnakes along the banks when going into or getting out of the water.

For these reasons and because of the limited floating opportunities, I've placed the Selway in this section of this guide. With criticism likely to come my way, I'll probably regret this decision. If you get a chance to float the Selway, take it. You won't be disappointed. Flies to use: Royal Wulff, Yellow Humpy, Elk Hair Caddis #14; Golden Stone #10; Dave's Hopper #8.

Warm River/Robinson Creek

If your idea of bliss is casting a dry fly in a stream loaded with 8- to 10-inch trout, the Warm River and Robinson Creek is your kind of place. Both enter the Henrys Fork at the town of Warm River east of Ashton, thus the name, "the Three Rivers Area."

The lower section of Warm River can be accessed from its confluence or by descending the bank from Highway 47. Ask directions from local fly shops if you plan to fish the upper end. Robinson Creek can also be accessed from Warm River or from Forest Road 241, upstream, that parallels and crosses the creek. Both rivers have good quantities of small fish. Horseshoe Lake, located east of these rivers can also be quite fun, but you will need a boat or float tube. Use standard attractor patterns in sizes #14–18 on all these waters.

Largemouth Bass.

Appendix

Idaho Fly Fishing Resources

Fly Fishing Shops

Southern Idaho

Blue Lakes Sporting Goods
1236 Blue Lakes Blvd. N.
Twin Falls, ID 83301
(208) 733-6446
www.bluelakesport.com

Jimmy's All Seasons Angler
275 A St.
Idaho Falls, ID 83402
(208) 524-7160
www.jimmysflyshop.com

Lee Aikin's Sport Shop
245 N. Main St.
Pocatello, ID 83201
(208) 233-3837

Simerly's General Store
280 S. Idaho St.
Wendell, ID 83355
(208) 536-6651

Northern Idaho

Black Sheep Sporting
    Goods
308 West Seale Ave.
Coeur d'Alene, ID 83815
(208) 667-7831
1701 Main St.
Lewiston, ID 83501
(208) 746-8948

Joe Roope's Castaway Fly
    Fishing Shop
350 W. Bosanko Ave.
Coeur d'Alene, ID 83815
(208) 765-3133
(800) 410-3133
www.
    castawayflyfishingshop.
    com

Western Idaho

Bear Creek Fly Shop
5622 W. State St.
Boise, ID 83703
(208) 853-8704

Howard's Fly Shoppe
1736 Garrity Blvd.
Nampa, ID 83687
(208) 467-7209
www.
    howardstackleshoppe.
    com/flyshop.htm

Stonefly Anglers
625 Vista Ave.
Boise, ID 83705
(208) 338-1333

The Idaho Angler
1682 S. Vista Ave.
Boise, ID 83705
(208) 389-9957
(800) 787-9957
www.idahoangler.com

Twin River Anglers
534 Thain Rd.
Lewiston, ID 83501
(208) 746-8946
www.traflyfish.com

Eastern Idaho

Henry's Fork Anglers
3340 Hwy. 20
Island Park, ID 83429
(208) 558-7525
(800) 788-4479
www.henrysforkanglers.com

Jimmy's All Season Angler
275 A St.
Idaho Falls, ID 83402
(208) 524-7160
www.jimmysflyshop.com

South Fork Lodge
P.0. Box 22
Swan Valley, ID 83449
(877) 347-4735
www.southforklodge.com

South Fork Outfitters
P. O. Box 22
Swan Valley, ID 83449
(800) 483-2110
www.southforkoutfitters.com

Trout Hunter on the
    Henry's Fork
3327 N. Hwy 20
Island Park, ID 83429
(208) 558-9900
www.trouthunt.com

Central Idaho

Bill Mason Outfitters
on the Sun Valley Mall
P.O. Box 127
Sun Valley, ID 83353
(208) 622-9305
www.billmasonoutfitters.com
bmoinfo@sunvalley.net

Lost River Outfitters
171 N Main
P.O. Box 3445
Ketchum, ID 83340
(208) 726-1706
www.lostriveroutfitters.com

McCoy's Tackle shop
Ace of Diamonds St.
P.O. Box 210
Stanley, ID 83278
(208) 774-3377

Silver Creek Outfitters
500 N. Main St.
P.O. Box 418
Ketchum, ID 83340
(208) 726-5282
(800) 732-5687
www.silver-creek.com

Sturtevants Mountain
    Outfitters
3400 N. Main
Ketchum, ID 83340
(208) 726-4501
www.sturtos.com

Montana

Blue Ribbon Flies
305 Canyon St.
W. Yellowstone, MT 59758
(406) 646-7642
www.blueribbonflies.com

Bud Lilly's Trout Shop
39 Madison Ave.
P.O. Box 530
W. Yellowstone, MT 59758
(406) 646-7801
(800) 854-9559
www.budlillys.com

Jacklin's Fly Shop
105 Yellowstone Ave.
P.O.Box 310
W. Yellowstone, MT 59758
(406) 646-7336
www.jacklinsflyshop.com

Madison River Fishing Co.
109 Main St.
P. O. Box 627
Ennis, MT 59729
(800) 227-7127
www.mrfc.com

Madison River Outfitters
117 Canyon St.
P.O. Box 398
W. Yellowstone, MT 59758
(406) 646-9644
(800) 646-9644
www.flyfishingyellowstone.com

The Tackle Shop
127 Main St.
P.O. Box 625
Ennis, MT 59729
(800) 808-2832
(406) 682-4263
www.thetackleshop.com

Wyoming

Westbank Anglers
3670 N. Moose-Wilson Rd.
P.O. Box 523
Teton Village, WY 83014
(307) 733-6483
(800) 922-3474
www.westbank.com

High Country Flies
185 N. Center
P.O. Box 3432
Jackson, WY 83001
(307) 733-7210
(866) 733-7210
www.flyfishingjacksonhole.com

Jack Dennis Sports
50 E. Broadway
P.O. Box 3369
Jackson, WY 83001
(307) 733-3270
(800) 570-3270
www.jackdennis.com

Orvis Jackson Hole
485 W. Broadway
P.O. Box 9029
Jackson, WY 83001
(307) 733-5407

Information Sources

Idaho Department of Fish and Game (IDFG)

Headquarters (IDFG)
P.O. Box 25
Boise, ID 83707
600 S. Walnut
Boise, ID 83712
(208) 334-3700
www.fishandgame.idaho.gov
www./fishandgame.idaho.gov/cms/about/offices

Clearwater Region (IDFG)
3316 16th St.
Lewiston, ID 83501
(208) 799-5010

Magic Valley Region (IDFG)
319 South 417 East
Jerome, ID 83338
(208) 324-4359

McCall Subregion (IDFG)
555 Deinhard Lane
McCall, ID 83638
(208) 634-8137

Panhandle Region (IDFG)
2750 Kathleen Ave.
Coeur d'Alene, ID 83814
(208) 769-1414

Salmon Region (IDFG)
99 Hwy 93 N.
P.O. Box 1336
Salmon, ID 83467
(208) 756-2271

Southeast Region (IDFG)
1345 Barton Rd.
Pocatello, ID 83204
(208) 232-4703

Southwest Region (IDFG)
3101 S. Powerline Rd.
Nampa, ID 83686
(208) 465-8465

Upper Snake Region (IDFG)
4279 Commerce Cir.
Idaho Falls, ID 83401
(208) 525-7290

Bureau of Land Management (BLM) District Offices

Idaho State Office (BLM)
1387 S. Vinnell Way
Boise, ID 83709
(208) 373-4000

Boise District (BLM)
3948 Development Ave.
Boise, ID 83705
(208) 384-3300

Coeur d'Alene District (BLM)
1808 N 3rd St.
Coeur d'Alene, ID 83814
(208) 769-5030

Idaho Falls District (BLM)
1405 Hollipark Dr.
Idaho Falls, ID 83401
(208) 524-7500

Twin Falls District (BLM)
378 Falls Ave.
Twin Falls, ID 83301
(208) 735-2060

Bureau of Land Management (BLM) Field Offices

Bruneau (BLM)
3948 Development Ave.
Boise, ID 83705
(208) 384-3300

Burley (BLM)
15 East 200 South
Burley, ID 83318
(208) 677-6641

Challis (BLM)
801 Blue Mountain Rd.
Challis, ID 83226
(208) 879-6200

Coeur d'Alene (BLM)
1808 N. 3rd St.
Coeur d'Alene, ID 83814
(208) 769-5030

Cottonwood (BLM)
Butte Dr., House One
Cottonwood, ID 83522
(208) 962-3245

Four Rivers (BLM)
3948 Development Ave.
Boise, ID 83705
(208) 384-3300

Jarbidge (BLM)
2620 Kimberly Rd.
Twin Falls, ID 83301
(208) 736-2350

Owyhee (BLM)
Street address pending
Marsing, ID 83639
(208) 384-3300

Pocatello (BLM)
1111 N. 8th Ave.
Pocatello, ID 83201
(208) 478-6340

Salmon (BLM)
50 Highway 93 South
Salmon, ID 83467
(208) 756-5400

Shoshone (BLM)
400 W. F St. (P.O. Box 2-B)
Shoshone, ID 83352
(208) 732-7200

Upper Snake (BLM)
1405 Hollipark Dr.
Idaho Falls, ID 83401
(208) 524-7500

USDA Forest Service Offices

http://www.fs.fed.us/recreation/map/state_list.shtml#Idaho

Boise National Forest
1249 South Vinnell Way, Suite 200
Boise, ID 83709
(208) 373-4100
/www.fs.fed.us/r4/boise

Caribou-Targhee National Forest
1405 Hollipark Dr.
Idaho Falls, ID 83401
(208) 524-7500
www.fs.fed.us/r4/caribou-targhee

Clearwater National Forest
12730 Highway 12
Orofino, ID 83544
(208)-476-4541
www.fs.fed.us/r1/clearwater

Nez Perce National Forest
Rte. 2 Box 475
Grangeville, ID 83530
(208) 983-1950
www.fs.fed.us/r1/nezperce

Payette National Forest
P.O. Box 1026
800 West Lakeside Ave.
McCall, ID 83638
(208) 634-0700
www.fs.fed.us/r4/payette

Salmon-Challis National
   Forest
50 Hwy 93 South
Salmon, ID 83467
(208) 756-5100
www.fs.fed.us/r4/sc

Sawtooth National Forest
2647 Kimberly Rd. E.
Twin Falls, ID 83301
(208) 737-3200
www.fs.fed.us/r4/sawtooth

Sawtooth National
   Recreation Area
Highway 75 (8 miles north
   of Ketchum)
Ketchum, ID 83340
Headquarters Visitor
   Center 208-727-5013
www.fs.fed.us/r4/
   sawtooth/recreation/
   recreport.htm

Bridger-Teton National
   Forest
P.O. Box 1888
Jackson, WY 83001
(307) 739-5500
http://www.fs.fed.us/btnf/

Wasatch-Cache National
   Forest
125 South State St.
Salt Lake City, UT 84138
(801) 236-3400
www.fs.fed.us/r4/wcnf/

Idaho Division of Tourism
   Development
PO Box 83720
700 W. State St.
Boise, ID 83720
(208) 334-2470
www.visitid.org

References and Resources

Idaho Department of Fish & Game

www.fishandgame.idaho.
   gov/cms/fish/

*Idaho Department of Fish
& Game General Fishing
Seasons and Rules*
www.fishandgame.idaho.
   gov/cms/fish/rules/

Idaho Atlas and Gazeteer,
   DeLorme Mapping

*Idaho's Top 30 Fishing
Waters,* Rendezvous
   Country Publications

*Idaho, Montana, Wyoming
Tour Book,* American
   Automobile Association

*Snake River Country Flies
and Waters,* Frank Amato
   Publications

Maps

Fish 'n Map Co.
www.fishnmap.com

Air Travel

American
www.aa.com
(800) 433-7300

America West
www.americawest.com
(800) 235-9292

Alaska
www.alaskaair.com
(800) 252-7522

Continental
www.continental.com
(800) 523-3273

Delta
www.delta.com
(800) 221-1212

Northwest
www.nwa.com
(800) 225-2525

Southwest
www.southwest.com
(800) 435-9792

United
www.united.com
(800) 241-6522

US Airways
www.usair.com
(800) 428-4322

Travel Agents

Expedia
www.expedia.com

Orbitz
www.orbitz.com

Priceline
www.priceline.com

Travelocity
www.travelocity.com

Organizations

Federation of Fly Fishers
National Headquarters
215 E. Lewis St.
Livingston, MT 59047
(406) 222-9369
Call for local club.
www.fedflyfishers.org

International Game
Fish Association
300 Gulf Stream Way
Dania Beach, FL 33004
(954) 927-2628
www.igfa.org

Trout Unlimited
(call for local chapter)
1300 North 17th St., #500
Arlington, VA 22209
(800) 834-2419
www.tu.org

Fly Fishing the Internet

www.amrivers.org
www.flyfish.com
www.flyfishing.com
www.flyfishamerica.com
www.flyfishingconnection.
   com
www.flyshop.com
www.frontierstravel.com
www.gssafaris.com
www.intlwomenflyfishers.
   org
www.ohwy.com
www.takemefishing.com

Knots

www.netknots.com

Where No Nonsense Guides Come From

No Nonsense guidebooks give you a quick, clear understanding of the essential information needed to fly fish a region's most outstanding waters. The authors are highly experienced and qualified local fly fishers. Maps are tidied versions of the author's sketches.

All who produce No Nonsense guides believe in providing top-quality products at a reasonable price. We also believe all information should be verified. We never hesitate to go out, fly rod in hand, to verify the facts and figures that appear in the pages of these guides. The staff is committed to this research. It's hard work, but we're glad to do it for you.

No Nonsense Fly Fishing Knots

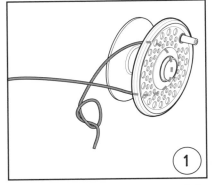
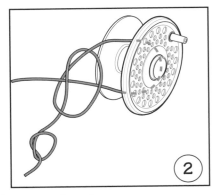
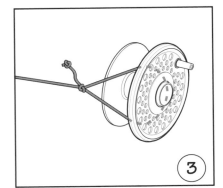

Arbor Knot: *Use this knot to attach backing to your fly reel.*

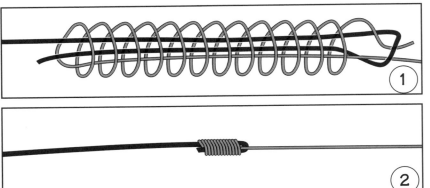
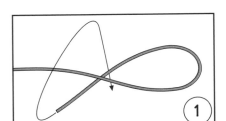

Albright Knot: *Use this knot to attach backing to your fly line.*

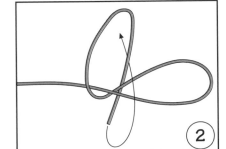

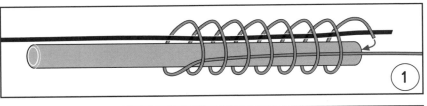

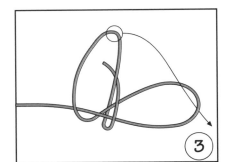

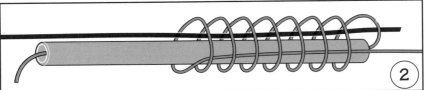

FLY LINE

LEADER

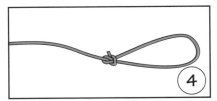

Nail Knot: *Use a nail, needle, or tube to tie this knot, which connects the forward end of the fly line to the butt end of the leader. Follow this with a Perfection Loop and you've got a permanent end loop that allows easy leader changes.*

Perfection Loop: *Use this knot to create a loop in the butt end of the leader for loop-to-loop connections.*

74

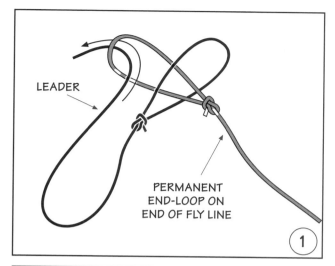

Loop-to-Loop: Easy connection of leader to a permanent monofilament end loop added to the tip of the fly line.

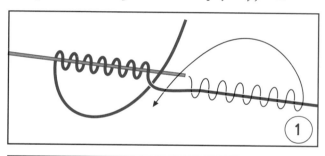

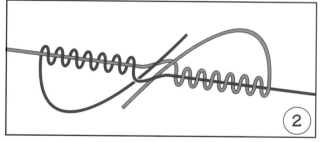

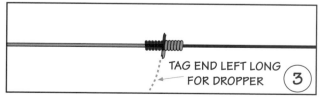

Blood Knot: Use this knot to connect sections of leader tippet material. Hard to tie but worth the effort.

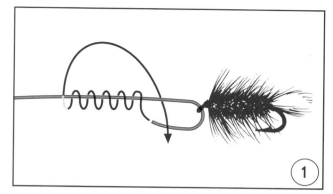

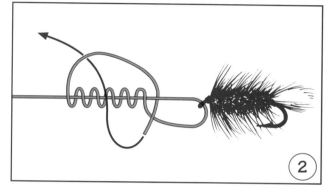

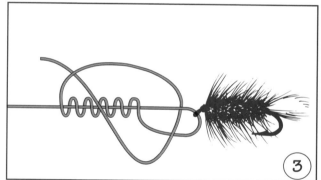

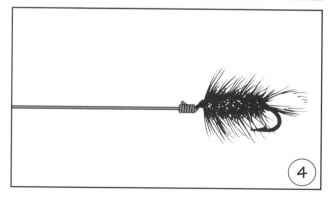

Improved Clinch Knot: Use this knot to attach the fly to the end of the tippet. Remember to moisten the knot before pulling it tight.

Find Your Way with These No Nonsense Guides

Fly Fishing Central and Southeastern Oregon
Harry Teel

The Metolius, Deschutes, McKenzie, Owyhee, John Day, and 35 other waters. Mr. Teel's 60 years of fly fishing went into the first No Nonsense fly fishing guide, published in 1993 and updated, expanded, and improved in 1998 by Jeff Perin. Now updated again in 2005 and bigger and better than ever.

ISBN #1-892469-09-X......................$19.95

Fly Fishing Colorado
Jackson Streit

Your experienced guide gives you the quick, clear understanding of the essential information you'll need to fly fish Colorado's most outstanding waters. Use this book to plan your Colorado fly fishing trip, and take this guide along for ready reference. Now in full color, this popular title has been updated and redesigned.

ISBN #1-892469-13-8......................$19.95

Fly Fishing New Mexico
Taylor Streit

Since 1970, Mr. Streit has been New Mexico's *foremost* fly fishing authority and professional guide. He's developed many fly patterns used throughout the region. Taylor owned the Taos Fly Shop for ten years and managed a bone fishing lodge in the Bahamas. He makes winter fly fishing pilgrimages to Argentina, where he escorts fly fishers and explorers.

ISBN #1-892469-04-9......................$18.95

Guide To Fly Fishing Nevada
Dave Stanley

Covers the Truckee, Walker, Carson, Eagle, Davis, and Ruby rivers, mountain lakes, and more. Mr. Stanley is recognized nationwide as the most knowledgeable fly fisher and outdoorsman in the state of Nevada. He owns and operates the Reno Fly Shop and Truckee River Outfitters in Truckee, California.

ISBN #0-9637256-2-9......................$18.95

Fly Fishing Utah
Steve Schmidt

yields extraordinary, uncrowded and little known fishing. Steve Schmidt, outfitter and owner of Western Rivers Flyfisher in Salt Lake City has explored these waters for more than 28 years. Covers fly fishing mountain streams and lakes, tailwaters, bass waters and reservoirs.

ISBN #0-9637256-8-8.....................$19.95

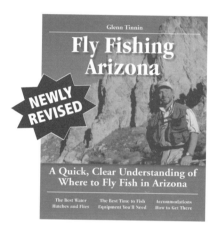

Fly Fishing Arizona
Glenn Tinnin

Arizona has a wonderful variety of waters to fly fish from the hot desert floor to cool alpine forests and higher! Here you'll find favorite trout waters from the famous Lees Ferry to small mountain lakes. Also included are some fine reservoirs and streams where you can fly fish.

ISBN #1-892469-02-2.......................$18.95

Fly Fishing Southern Baja
Gary Graham

With this book you can fly to Baja, rent a car, and go out on your own to find exciting saltwater fly fishing! Mexico's Baja Peninsula is now one of the premier destinations for saltwater fly anglers.

ISBN #1-892469-00-6.....................$18.95

Fly Fishing California
Ken Hanley

Coming Soon: Mr. Hanley and some very talented contributors, like Jeff Solis, Dave Stanley, Katie Howe, and others, have fly fished nearly every top water in California. From saltwater to high mountains, bass to steelhead—they provide all you need to discover the best places to fly fish in the Golden State.

ISBN #1-892469-10-3........................$TBD

Fly Fishing Lees Ferry, 2nd Edition
Dave Foster

This colorful guide provides a clear understanding of the complex and fascinating 15 miles of river that can provide fly anglers 40-fish days. Detailed maps direct fly and spin fishing access. Learn history, boating, and geology and see the area's beauty. Indispensable for the angler and intrepid visitor to Marble Canyon.

ISBN 1-892469-15-4 ....$18.95

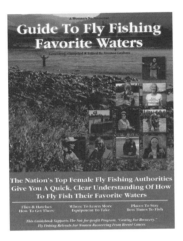

A Woman's Guide to Fly Fishing Favorite Waters
Yvonne Graham

Forty-five of the top women fly fishing experts reveal their favorite waters. From scenic spring creeks in the East to big trout waters in the Rockies to exciting Baja, all are described from the female perspective. A major donation goes to Casting for Recovery, a nonprofit organization for women recovering from breast cancer.

ISBN #1-892469-03-0 ....$19.95

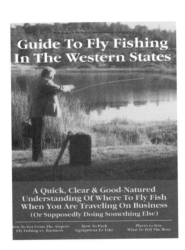

Business Traveler's Guide to Fly Fishing in the Western States
Bob Zeller

A seasoned road warrior reveals where one can fly fish within a two-hour drive of every major airport in 13 western states. Don't miss another day of fishing!

ISBN #1-892469-01-4 ....$18.95

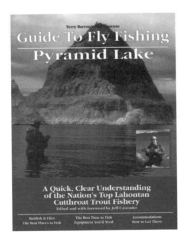

Guide To Fly Fishing Pyramid Lake, Nevada
Terry Barron

The Gem of the Desert is full of huge Lahontan cutthroat trout. Terry has recorded everything you need to fly fish the most outstanding trophy cutthroat fishery in the United States. Where else can you get tired of catching 18"–25" trout?

ISBN #0-9637256-3-7 ....$15.95

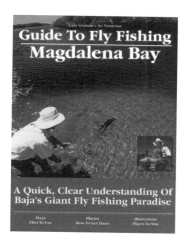

Guide To Fly Fishing Magdalena Bay
Gary Graham

Guide and excursion leader Gary Graham (*Baja on the Fly*) lays out the truth about snook in mangroves, off-shore marlin, calving whales from Alaska, beautiful birds, kayaking, even surfing. With photos, illustrations, maps, and travel information, this is "the Bible" for this unique region.

ISBN #1-892469-08-1 ....$24.95

Seasons of the Metolius
John Judy

Learn how a beautiful riparian environment both changes and stays the same over the years. This look at nature comes from a man who makes his living working in nature and chronicles John Judy's 30 years of study, writing, and fly fishing his beloved home water, the crystal-clear Metolius River in central Oregon.

ISBN #1-892469-11-1 ....$20.95

State of Idaho
Major Highway Network

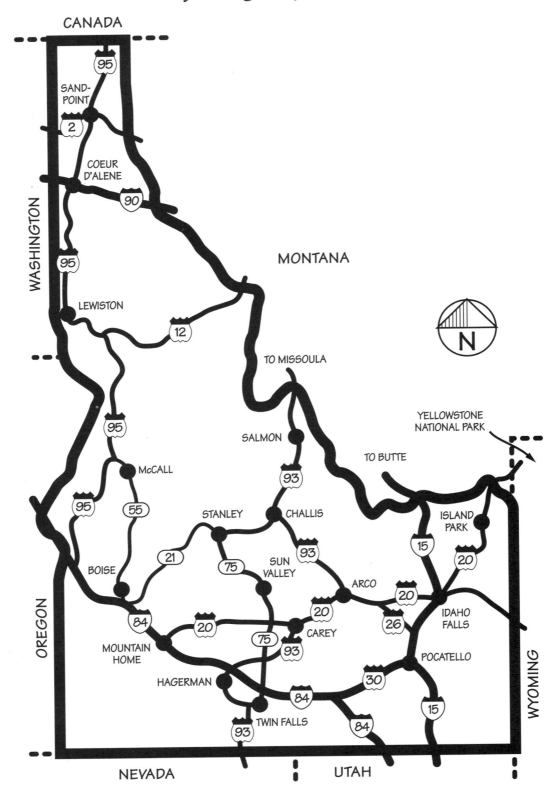